THE 7 ELEMENTS OF STRATEGY EXECUTION

THE 7 ELEMENTS OF STRATEGY EXECUTION

CREATING A CULTURE THAT WILL ENSURE STRATEGY SUCCESS

by Mona Mitchell and David Barrett

First Edition

Published by

KEBS Publishing, Collingwood, Ontario

The 7 Elements of Strategy Execution
Creating a Culture That Will Ensure Strategy Success

Authors: Mona Mitchell and David Barrett
Editors: Kelly Jones and Simon Doyle

Cover Design: cityzenpower

Published by:
KEBS Publishing
Collingwood, Ontario

Production © 2018 by KEBS Publishing
ISBN-10: 1986931587
ISBN-13: 978-1986931588

CONTENTS

DEDICATIONS

T *his book has been a dream of mine for many years and I am so thrilled to share it with you. I dedicate this book to my late father, Sam Younan, whose profound teachings and support will never be forgotten.*

To my colleagues at ACHIEVEBLUE, I am thankful for your support and commitment. Myrna thank you for starting me on this journey. And I particularly want to thank my husband David for always believing in me.

Mona Mitchell

****

I dedicate this book to all of my colleagues, past and present, at The Schulich Executive Education Centre. We started our relationship 22 years ago and it remains a critical part of my life today. Thank you for your support and encouragement. And to Elaine Gutmacher and the late Peter Zarry, thank you for believing in me.

David Barrett

FOREWARD

In a world of constant change and disruption many, many, books inform us of what we should be doing but too few help us understand how to get there. With the old 'command and control' structures failing to meet the demands of needed innovation and agility, organization leaders know they have to change, but how? We are inundated with stories and research about how we must break down silos, listen more to employees and especially the millennials, adopt better technology and especially AI, work more closely with strategic allies, suppliers and partners to build effective networks, and still achieve ambitious commercial goals but in ways that are pro-active ethically and sustainably.

Tall order huh?

As the authors of this book know it is not just being clear where to go but how to get there. The founding principles behind this book are that execution is often more important than strategy and an organization's culture is often more important than its structure in achieving effective execution.

The great business writer Alfred Chandler in his research concluded that structure should follow strategy. Yet too often we use the lens and knowledge of existing structures to view the world and thereby fail to see opportunities and threats. Lou Gerstner the ex-CEO of IBM observed "culture isn't just one aspect of the game, it is the game", yet too often we fail to engage our most valuable resource, our staff, in the journey through disruption and change.

According to both the World Economic Forum (WEF) Competitiveness Report 2017/18 and IMD's World Competitiveness Yearbook 2017 Canada is really poor at investing in upgrading the skills of its staff: a key to building a strong culture and executional excellence. Canada ranks 20th out of 63 countries in the IMD survey on the importance placed on upgrading workforce skills, and in the WEF survey 23rd out of 137 countries in the extent of staff training. Both directly impact Canada's poor innovation and competitiveness accomplishments.

So our authors are on to the right topics to be of use to us: how to achieve more effective execution of our strategic direction. In plain English, avoiding too many consulting buzzwords, yet with valid research references, they give us 7 interrelated elements that can be combined to overcome 'failure to execute'. These elements: Clarity, Commitment, The Team, Accountability, Synergy, The Plan and Leadership are analyzed and discussed in a clear, concise manner designed to help the reader develop a coherent plan of action to improve execution. The focus on how to make the best use of human capital and the need to investigate new methods of organizing like Holocracy, all build to the most important of goals which is to maximize valuable employee engagement to achieve a high performance culture.

New global competitors like Alibaba of China 'get' this. Jack Ma and his team at Alibaba have created an organization that in vision, strategy, structure and employee profile and practice are well equipped to achieve their goal of becoming the 5th largest economy in the world. Organizations like Alibaba are already following, indeed leading, application of most of the principles that this book covers. Here in Canada we need our organizations to step up and implement these practices if we are to have any chance to compete globally, or indeed domestically in the future. Mona Mitchell and David Barrett have done a great job in synthesizing and integrating good research and personal experience in producing a reader-friendly roadmap to improved executional performance.

Don't just read and think about their findings, we need you to take action and implement them.....build a strong organization culture and deliver exceptional execution please!

Alan Middleton PhD, Executive Director, Schulich Executive Education Centre and Distinguished Adjunct Professor of Marketing, Schulich School of Business, York University.

INTRODUCTION

This book is not about how to develop a brilliant strategic plan. While it's critical that you have a solid strategy, we apologize in advance: We're not here to help you create one.

But, we are here to aid significantly with your strategy execution. What we will do is empower you with the ability to execute your strategic plan. For some companies, it looks so easy. They're rolling out the strategy, communicating it to team members, meeting the plan's targets – and everyone's having fun doing it. That's solid execution. If only all organizations could achieve that. The problem is that leaders tend to focus much more on creating the strategic plan than on executing it. Execution is just as important as the strategy itself – if not more important – yet too often execution stalls. We have heard from too many senior executives about how their strategic plans have ended up on a shelf. They develop a solid strategy, put the right processes, people and technology in place to support it, but the plan goes nowhere. The gears are jammed. That's why we wrote this book. We explore why execution stalls and how to avoid it.

Right off the top, we'll tell you what's likely holding back your execution. It's how your people think and behave – it's your organizational culture. Many people hear the term *organizational culture* and their eyes glaze over. It's too abstract and wooly. It's too mysterious and complex. It's intangible, they think, so they move on to dealing with easier problems related to organizational process and structure. Well, we're excited to tell you that organizational culture is not as difficult a problem as you may have thought. There is a body of well-refined practical research and experience that clearly outlines how to shape and sustain a powerful, high-performance culture. Whether you like it or not, your organization has a culture. In this book, we provide practical ways to shape and influence it.

We've seen the connection between outcomes and how employees interpret and operationalize goals. Execution comes from the thousands of decisions, big and small, that employees make each day.[1] They make those decisions within some type of organizational culture, whether it's constructive, defensive, high-performance or dysfunctional. You can have the right technology, processes and targets set up to execute your strategy, but, if your culture is off, your people will take it nowhere. More often than not, the degree to which an organization's strategy is successful is determined by its culture.

Culture is the often-overlooked foundation of an organization. It determines how the group retains talent, how it develops and releases new products and whether it meets targets. It affects how happy and satisfied employees are at work. Your people are the force behind the execution of your strategy, and if they're not thinking and behaving in ways that advance your goals, you've got a culture problem. Unfortunately, executives often ignore, misunderstand or are unaware of their culture until they realize that their organization is in peril. They become like the firefighters of Pompeii, dousing small flames while disaster looms above.

This book provides a concise, prescriptive analysis of the links between strategy execution and organizational culture. We've compiled our own primary source research. Published here for the first time are exclusive interviews with executives who discuss best practices supporting a high-performance culture and whose insights reinforce our analysis. We break down strategy execution into the following seven essential elements so that you, as CEO or organizational leader, can build a high-performance culture and kick your strategic plan into action.

---

[1] Gary L. Neilson, Karla L. Martin and Elizabeth Powers, "The Secrets to Successful Strategy Execution," *Harvard Business Review*, June 2008 (accessed July 12, 2017). Available at https://hbr.org/2008/06/the-secrets-to-successful-strategy-execution.

ELEMENT 1: CLARITY

Clarity is clear seeing. We describe how strategy execution requires that your people understand the goals ahead of them, how to get there and why they're being asked to do what they need to do. Clarity is a shared understanding of what goals need to be reached, what tasks need to be accomplished and why, all supported by excellent communications. Everything within the organization, from expected behaviors to processes, are aligned with the objectives of the group.

ELEMENT 2: COMMITMENT

Targeted tools, processes and rewards will help you generate and nurture commitment from employees. Team members must believe in the strategy. You want team members who are committed to the strategy, their colleagues and the organization, and who understand what's in it for them and the company. They come in to work every day energized and focused. This is commitment. We discuss how to build and cultivate it.

ELEMENT 3: THE TEAM

Your organization is your people, and it's your people who execute the strategy. This element focuses on having the right people in the right roles and hiring for fit with the organization's ideal culture – that is, the culture your organization is trying to achieve. We discuss the importance of building strong team-oriented and collaborative attitudes.

ELEMENT 4: ACCOUNTABILITY

Accountability is trust and open communications. It contributes to a constructive culture where employees feel free to hold the CEO accountable for what they do or say, just as senior leaders hold employees accountable. People in your organization should feel accountable to one another and supported by their colleagues. Leaders play a critical role ensuring people understand accountability and that they are empowered to deliver on their goals.

ELEMENT 5: SYNERGY

Synergy is linking it all together. It's ensuring resources, infrastructure and capacity are in place to empower your people and your organization's constructive culture to flourish. When a high-performance culture takes hold, execution can happen faster and more swiftly than expected, exceeding targets and results. This the effect of synergy: The elements come together to create an effect that's greater than the sum of its parts.

ELEMENT 6: THE PLAN

A strategic plan is a solid road map, but how will you follow it? Your strategic plan must be complemented with a plan of execution. This plan includes a vision, values and a set of goals – all aligned with one another as well as with the culture and strategy.

ELEMENT 7: LEADERSHIP

Leaders, and their leadership by example, are vital to strategy execution. A high-performance culture craves superb leadership. Your people need and want to know what's expected of them. Leaders must show by example and demonstrate ideal behaviors. They facilitate independent decision-making. They work with employees to help them grow, learn and achieve personal success.

BRINGING IT ALL TOGETHER

Strategy execution is what you get when the seven elements come together. An organization with aligned vision, values and goals, ownership of tasks at all levels, and a structure of accountability and reward is one that has successfully executed its strategic plan. Employees at all levels promote principles that lead to positive action and reinforce a constructive, achievement-oriented culture. Command-and-control organizational models may get results over the short term but, over time, the culture can break down and become dysfunctional. Employees are not motivated when they must take on tasks for which they feel no ownership. What drives people is personal success and making a contribution. In the coming pages, we describe how to use a culture model to bring your strategy to life – and achieve outstanding results you hadn't thought possible.

CHAPTER 1
STRATEGIC PLANNING 201: THE EXECUTION PHASE (OR THE PART WE ALL FORGET ABOUT)

WHAT'S THE PROBLEM?

Do your strategic plans, your projects, get stuck? Do they have a tendency to seize up? Let us illustrate. Charlie is a new vice president of sales training hired by a large pharmaceutical company. His job is to introduce a new selling technique to recently hired pharmaceutical representatives. He puts together a two-week onboarding program to teach sales reps new ways of working with doctors and pharmacists. The planned program has extraordinary potential, and three months is given to the sales reps to activate their acquired skills and knowledge.

But something gets stuck. After the three months, Charlie accompanies the reps on calls across the country to observe and coach performance. No matter what city or doctor's office he finds himself in, none of what was taught is evident. In coffee meetings with the reps, Charlie asks, "What happened? You were so excited about the training." They all respond that, once they got into the field, district managers told them, "Forget what head office told you. That's not how we do business around here."

Clearly, there's a problem here. Not one member of the sales teams challenged their managers by implementing what they learned and giving them an opportunity to assess whether the change would be an improvement. Why did the sales reps not contest management? Why did they keep their mouths shut instead of confronting the status quo? Unfortunately, as Charlie learned, it wasn't within the corporate behavior to do so. Somehow, somewhere, this good strategic plan got stuck. What's the problem?

FAILURE TO EXECUTE

Let's talk about goals and how organizations set out to achieve them. All organizations have goals. You could even say that's their starting point. It's goals, and the novel ideas behind them, that lead to the creation of organizations and start-ups. Apple Inc.'s goal was to introduce home computing. Ford's was to make the automobile the future of transportation. For most organizations, goals are less ambitious. They are high-level outcomes such as profitability, client loyalty, employee engagement, innovation and market leadership. All organizations are created and sustained by defined goals. Whatever the objectives, goals must be clear and precise enough that their achievement can be measured in degrees.

With clear goals, planning and initiatives are possible. Operations, processes and resources can be implemented as the supporting infrastructure. A formal vision and strategy are articulated to meet a strategic objective and embrace a loftier mission. The vision defines how the group or company views the world and the marketplace. Strategic planning may include how to move into identified markets, levels of market penetration, organizational positioning, revenues, time frames and high-level tactics for achievement. In other words, a plan is formulated.

In an effort to reach goals, leaders tend to put a great amount of emphasis on what we call organizational climate, investing energy, time and money to build an optimized infrastructure. They organize business functions into efficient reporting structures and delegate authorities and accountabilities. They review government and industry regulations to ensure compliance is incorporated into the company fabric. Necessary skills and competencies are mapped against business functions to produce optimal job descriptions and career ladders. Professional development programs are established, and core business principles are translated into formal policies and informal employee guidelines. Product and project management are harmonized with market research, sales and production. New technologies are sourced, tested and implemented. Overall, a lot of effort goes in to the infrastructure to support the achievement of goals. This infrastructure, while important, creates a surface-level organizational climate. The problem is that leaders often mistakenly believe that organizational climate will achieve outcomes.

Back to Charlie. He, and the leaders who developed his strategic plan, realize their objectives aren't being reached. The leaders rightfully pose a host of questions: What is causing this ongoing performance gap? Do we have the right people? Have we invested enough in the right technology? Have we provided sufficient direction and organizational support for operations? Why does our competitor, who essentially has the same structures and systems, do so much better? Why do our people keep leaving to work for the competition, when they're paid the same? We know we're missing something critical. What is it? Why did the strategic plan fail to get off the ground?

Ann Barnes, President & CEO MedData explains: "I believe that strategic plans require passion from the leader and the team. Often ideas and plans sound very good and from a business standpoint make great sense, however, the leadership team that needs to drive it don't feel it. They need to internalize the plan and then with great passion drive the progress and completion of the plan. It is very difficult to create plans that the leaders can truly internalize but when you do the team can't be stopped! Success is inevitable at that point!"[2]

What these leaders have is a failure in execution because they did not engage those that were to drive it and did not create the passion required to drive the plan so what they got was – a

---

[2] Ann Barnes President and CEO MedData, interview with authors (October 2017).

failure to execute the strategic plan. For companies that have solid organizational climates in place, there are two very common reasons for this. One is that the strategy was a bad idea from the outset (for example, a company pens a new strategy to expand its chain of snowmobile stores into Mexico). So, first of all, a successful strategic plan must be sensible. Perhaps the plan is to launch a new product, acquire another player in the market or expand to another jurisdiction. We assume here that you have a sensible strategic plan – strategy failure based on a bad idea is not what this book is about. Rather, this book is about Charlie and his problem, which brings us to the second most-common way a strategy fails: When the organization has a strong strategy, plan and organizational climate implemented but it can't get things done. It can't execute the plan.

Unfortunately, it's a problem that's far too common. Strategy execution researcher Donald Sull, senior lecturer at the Massachusetts Institute of Technology Sloan School of Management, has reported with other researchers on a survey of more than four hundred CEOs around the world that "executional excellence" ranked as the executives' top corporate challenge. The results presented that the companies surveyed in Asia, Europe and the United States ranked execution as the most important challenge among a list of 80 issues, including innovation, geopolitical instability and top-line growth.[3] The good news is that you're not alone. The bad news is that, around the globe, companies' ability to execute clearly needs improvement.

WHY CAN'T I EXECUTE ON MY STRATEGY?

Execution is the activity that bridges goals and results. Unfortunately, there are many ways it can get stuck. Perhaps the goals aren't clear. Perhaps there's bad communication and team members aren't singing from the same songbook. Maybe

---

[3] Donald Sull, Rebecca Homkes and Charles Sull, "Why Strategy Execution Unravels—and What to Do About It," *Harvard Business Review*, March 2015 (accessed July 16, 2016). Available at https://hbr.org/2015/03/why-strategy-execution-unravelsand-what-to-do-about-it.

leaders are setting bad examples or rewarding behaviors that run counter to the strategy. What we explain in this book is how all of these things are part of the number one reason organizations fail to execute their strategy. It comes down to this ethereal thing called organizational culture. Shake your head, but what we're talking about is very real. Organizational culture is the underpinning for the success of an organization's strategic goal.

Organization are not only made up of processes, objectives and results. Sure, these are part of the organization's fabric but, really, companies are made up of people. And it's the actions and behaviors of these people that shape and perpetuate the organization's culture. To fit in and succeed, employees must align themselves with this collective culture".

Many organizations fail to invest in a culture that makes the best use of their human capital as they strive to execute the strategic plan. Instead, major investments in policy, technical competency and reporting structures are made in isolation – and with less-than-desirable results. Leaders restructure again and again, rearranging hierarchies to find a better place for the buck to stop. Unfortunately, the measures address the symptoms of organizational failure, not the underlying cause. When everything appears to be in place and functioning well yet there's still a significant performance gap, it's time to look at the organizational culture. Unsurprisingly, culture can also explain the inverse: Some companies see a performance surplus when aspects of their organizational climate, such as business processes or technology, are lacking capabilities. Their people are exceeding the organization's process and technology gaps.

Culture isn't part of your organization, it *is* your organization. And it can impede, even halt, the execution of your strategy. Executives must be honest with themselves and ask whether the behaviors within their organization are the kind that will bridge goals and results. Does the communication advance the strategy? Is the company dominated by silos that rarely collaborate or trust each other? Are employees focused on protecting their jobs until the economy turns around? Is productivity suffering because top people are no longer sure what's expected of them? Are leaders setting the right examples?

Robert MacLellan, chairman of Northleaf Capital Partners and former chief investment officer for TD Bank Group, explains: "I think there are lots of times when you can have a strategic plan that's guaranteed to fail. They can be guaranteed to fail because they're simply not implementable within the competitive nature of the industry that you're in. Or they can fail because you can't get the buy-in of the individuals who are part of your senior management team; or the frontline staff, for one reason or another, can't be persuaded to buy in."[4] This buy-in that leaders seek isn't easy to get. If it were easy, every leader would be doing it. But we're about to break it down for you and show you how to achieve it. The answers to motivating people and getting buy-in lie within the culture.

WHAT DOES MY CULTURE LOOK LIKE IF IT'S NOT EXECUTING?

For most organizations, execution of their strategy gets caught up in an unclear vision and goals. Organizations usually find it difficult to state their short-, mid - and long-term goals clearly enough to execute them. Worse, the organization hasn't set out any goals at all. Unclear goals are typically brought on by a focus on short-term objectives and results (for example, financial or sales targets) driven by the leadership team. The pattern generates an *action du jour* mentality that derails strategy execution.

Employees are smart. They can see when an organization sacrifices its strategy for the easier route of quick actions that get the daily job done in the short term. They notice very quickly whether the company's strategy goes out the window as soon as they run up against barriers. What follows is a culture of hand-to-mouth survival tactics and crisis intervention. Senior leaders become directly involved in operational issues and,

---

[4] Robert MacLellan, interview with the authors (March 2016).

with a less efficient organization, a backlog of work faced by everyone grinds down the company, not to mention its people. While everyone is bailing out the boat, there's no one steering or watching the horizon. The strategic plan is forgotten.

This is an organization whose strategy, goals, culture and organizational climate are not aligned. There is a clear disconnect between staff and departments. One symptom is a lack of collaboration – even between senior leaders. Instead, they make defensive decisions that protect their positions, team members and departments. The leaders sometimes possess very good relationships with the president or CEO on an individual level, making the executive feel comfortable with the disconnect and lack of collaboration.

The symptoms above indicate a host of problems with the culture. They tend to come with several related issues, such as team leaders who compete with one another or leaders who create fear and fail to take accountability for their actions. Instead, they protect their turf and seek power and influence, effecting a decline in teamwork within the organization. In such a case, leaders focus on their own area of the business, feeling they are neither paid nor encouraged to be concerned about other departments unless an issue impacts them directly. The culture is a defensive one, driving a fear-based environment rather than a collaborative one. In many cases, employees disengage and dysfunction and infighting sets in. In any case, execution is impeded as the organization's broader objectives fall by the wayside.

It doesn't have to be this way. This book discusses how and why to build a culture of strong execution within your organization. Your culture can be developed so that your people drive the organization to get things done, execute your strategic plan and bridge goals and results. In the chapters to come, we outline the seven elements of a high-performance culture.

CHAPTER 2
WHY SHOULD I CARE?

THE COST OF POOR OR NO EXECUTION

Still wondering why you should care about a high-performance culture that gets things done? From raising your productivity and performance to running a more positive, healthier place to work, there are many benefits. Perhaps you simply want to remove some behaviors from within your organization that are impeding your goals. It's certainly true that over time some cultures can become dysfunctional. If that's the case, and you've recognized it, why not work on removing that dysfunction? Dysfunction comes from dysfunctional behaviors. As executive coach and author Marshall Goldsmith famously observed: "After living with their dysfunctional behavior for so many years (a sunk cost if ever there was one), people become invested in defending their dysfunctions rather than changing them."[5] Dysfunction in its own right is a big enough cost. How much time and energy does your organization put into defending it?

i) The Bottom Line

Perhaps one of the biggest reasons to concern yourself with execution is your bottom line. There is plenty of literature linking execution and profitability.[6] Organizations with solid

---

[5] Natalie J. Sayer and Bruce Williams, *Lean for Dummies* (Hoboken, N.J.: John Wiley & Sons, 2012), 67.

[6] See, e.g., Larry Bossidy, Ram Charan and Charles Burck, *Execution: The Discipline of Getting Things Done* (New York: Crown Business, 2002); and Robert S. Kaplan and David P. Norton, *The Execution Premium: Linking Strategy to Opera-*

execution are focused, their teams aligned toward their goals. A performance culture affects your earnings in many ways, but, at a basic level, your organization as a whole is more effective. It can set goals and, more important, achieve them. If your organization can't effectively execute plans, what is it doing? Unfortunately, bright ideas don't pay off in themselves. What if Albert Einstein never published any of his ideas? What if Apple Inc. designed the perfect iPhone prototype but never tested it or got it to market?

Research by Myrna Ain, founding partner at ACHIEVEBLUE Corporation has established links between leadership, culture and performance. The research involved in-person interviews and psychometric surveys with CEOs and employees from 43 of Canada's best-managed companies. The companies surveyed had the highest rates of employee satisfaction, indicating positive, high-performance cultures. The research found that these organizations with constructive cultures increased revenues by 682% over an 11-year period, while net incomes rose by 756%. Those results contrasted with companies that had "defensive" cultures – that is, employees with more passive behaviors and "don't rock the boat" attitudes. Their results? Revenues rose 166% over the same period, while profits gained 1%.[7] Willis Towers Watson (previously Towers Perrin) similarly conducted a global survey of tens of thousands of employees in 2006 and found that companies with engaged, high-performance workforces had a 52% operating income performance gap over companies with low employee engagement.[8] Engaged employees translates into teams who are executing. How do you engage your employees? That's what the following chapters are about: how you can change

---

tions for Competitive Advantage (Boston: Harvard Business School Publishing, 2008).

[7] ACHIEVEBLUE Corporation, "The Best of the Best: The Role of Leadership and Culture in Creating Canada's Best Organizations," research paper presented to Conference Board of Canada (Updated November 2008).

[8] KPMG, "The Real Value of Engaged Employees," KPMG, 2012 (accessed March 2, 2017). Available at www.kpmg.com/US/en/IssuesAndInsights/ArticlesPublications/Documents/real-value-of-engaged-employees.pdf

team members' behaviors and how you can effectively inspire team members to embrace your organization's expectations and improve their behaviors"?

With poor execution, there are very obvious costs related to sales and profits, and there are additional secondary costs related to efficiency and use of resources. The cost of not executing isn't reflective in sales numbers. It also comes through lost opportunities. Organizations that are not executing their long-term plans tend to struggle with day-to-day management issues and difficulties with personnel. While management and entire teams are playing catch-up or trying to correct errors in execution, what opportunities have been missed? Your teams must have the space and focus available to them to see opportunities and take advantage of them. Where there's dysfunction, there's lost potential in new products and services that may be delayed or, worse, that may never come to market.

ii) Employee Engagement

Employee engagement is tremendously powerful and has an enormous impact on productivity. Your employees' commitment relates directly to both high workplace satisfaction and the organization's ability to execute strategy. Unsurprisingly, engagement also has a direct relationship with overall performance. Studies on employee engagement consistently link the engagement and retention of talent to bottom-line business performance. Ask yourself: When your employees come to work, do they really come to work?

Apparently, not enough leaders are asking this question, or doing enough about it. Many companies and organizations are suffering from the consequences of low employee engagement. Towers Watson conducted a survey of thirty-two thousand employees in 2014 and found that only four in 10 employees are highly engaged.[9] Failure to execute is a significant cost, but –

---

[9] Towers Watson, "The 2014 Global Workforce Study: Driving Engagement Through a Consumer-Like Experience," Towers Watson, August 2014 (accessed

putting that aside – a disengaged workforce also leads to substantial direct expenses related to staff turnover. The CEB Corporate Leadership Council's surveys on employee engagement indicate that engaged employees are 87% less likely to leave their jobs than those who aren't engaged.[10] We should not underestimate how much it costs your organization each time an employee leaves and a replacement must be hired. It's estimated to take between 18 and 24 months to recover the costs of one recruitment, leading the U.S. Bureau of Labor Statistics to calculate a stunning figure for annual turnover costs in the United States: $5 trillion.[11] These expenses are completely unnecessary and avoidable. An engaged team, an attendant benefit of a high-performance culture, avoids these costs.

iii) Drawing the Best and Brightest

Most organizations struggle with talent recruitment, whether they acknowledge it or not. Finding new people isn't difficult – but finding the right person, the most talented person, is. And retaining your most talented team members is another challenge. In years gone by, you might have heard a manager say, "We can always get more where they came from" or "They better get on board." Those days are long gone. Drawing the best and brightest is more challenging as organizations hire from younger demographic groups, whose expectations are radically different than those of previous generations. The talented millennial generation, and now Gen Z, demand much higher standards from employers. They want to understand the company's values. They research what your company stands for, first online and then again during the interview. If things seem off, they vote with their feet.

March 2, 2017). Available at www.towerswatson.com/en-CA/Insights/IC-Types/Survey-Research-Results/2014/08/the-2014-global-workforce-study.
[10] KPMG, "The Real Value of Engaged Employees," KPMG, 2011 (accessed March 10, 2017) Available at https://www.kpmg.com/US/en/IssuesAndInsights/ArticlesPublications/Documents/real-value-of-engaged-employees.pdf.
[11] Bureau of Labor Statistics, "State of the Global Workforce," United States Department of Labor, 2013

Software company SAS Institute Inc. has built strong employee engagement on its culture objective of employee happiness. Company perks – from a discounted daycare, a pool, a health-care center and free work-life counseling – are intended to be symbolic yet very real reminders that its people matter to SAS. The company values its people and communicates this to them. While employees may use the services on its campus at any time during the workday, most people are, in fact, working more than the required 35 hours per week. It's not about hours. It's about independence, contribution, trust, collaboration and flexibility. The approach has gone a long way to improve the company's retention and turnover rate, which has remained below 3%.[12]

The ability to attract, develop and retain younger generations of talented professionals is an important indicator for the long-term success of organizations. Being a "great place to work" – not just in espoused values but in your real organizational culture – is a key attraction. Potential candidates can detect when a company's employees aren't engaged, when its culture isn't aligned with its values. Younger generations are tapped in to social media networks, which are playing a bigger role in word-of-mouth marketing and help them find the right places to work and avoid organizations with lesser reputations. An organization that isn't executing, isn't motivating its employees, and it can't honestly promote the view that its most valuable resource is its people. The New York–based Conference Board estimates that more than half of Americans are unhappy in their jobs,[13] and it is these organizations that are not executing – and they are less competitive. There are direct

---

[12] Mark C. Crowley, "How SAS Became the World's Best Place to Work," Fast Company, Jan. 22, 2013 (accessed March 10, 2017). Available at www.fastcompany.com/3004953/how-sas-became-worlds-best-place-work.

[13] The Conference Board Ben Cheng, Michelle Kan, Gad Levanon, Ph.D., and Rebecca L. Ray, Ph.D. as per www.conference-board.org/publications/publicationdetail.cfm?publicationid=2785&centerId=4?], "Job Satisfaction: 2014 Edition," The Conference Board, June 2014 (accessed March 15, 2017). Available at www.conference-board.org/publications/publicationdetail.cfm?publicationid=2785.

links between high-performance organizational cultures that get things done and being a great place to work.

iv) Cultural Disconnect

There are additional costs when you have what we call a cultural disconnect. This disconnect is the gap between the espoused values of a company and the real behaviors within its organizational culture. The costs go beyond the organization's ability to attract and retain the best and brightest, as discussed earlier. A cultural disconnect can lead to all kinds of unforeseen problems and project and team failures. For instance, an organization's devotion to perfection in its products, as described in its corporate values and marketing, may be at odds with lackadaisical oversight and accountability in design and assembly. This is a cultural disconnect – behaviors do not align with espoused values. The gap can also become apparent between the rhetoric of leaders and the actual behaviors of leaders and team members. When these gaps or cultural disconnects emerge and grow, employees disengage.

The larger the gap between the espoused values and the real culture of the organization, the stronger the impact. These cultural disconnects have a profoundly negative impact on strategic outcomes, such as profitability, client loyalty and innovation. Employees increasingly disengage, failing to get on board with new initiatives or strategic plans. Organizations start to see the opposite of a performance culture: Instead of moving projects ahead toward goals, employees actually inhibit or impede them. The situation is made worse if a corporation implements cost cutting or other efficiencies – say, due to changing market conditions – while it has an internal cultural disconnect. Management's impetus for change may be well-intentioned but, with a lack of trust within the culture, they are simply magnifying employee dissatisfaction. Employee buy-in is far off. In fact, staff are more than withdrawn: They start to work *against* the very changes sought by management.

BUILDING A BETTER ORGANIZATION

What's not to like about building a better organization? It's one of the many advantages of developing a culture focused on executing the strategic plan. This is an organization where employees are satisfied in their work, take pride in accomplishing tasks and thrive in teamwork. Its people exude the organization's values, which spreads into support for its reputation and competitiveness.

i) Healthier Work Environment

There is a direct relationship between the kind of execution we describe in this book and organizations that invest in their people. These are organizations that maintain constructive, robust and productive cultures and whose investments in their team members translate into efficiency, productivity and better results. These are not sunk costs. These high-performing organizations get far more out of a happier and more satisfied group of employees. They report high levels of employee motivation and loyalty, increased team cohesiveness, effectiveness and other improved efficiencies.[14]

Daniel H. Pink, author of *Drive: The Surprising Truth about What Motivates Us*, writes that employees want autonomy, expertise and engagement. When this is channeled into the strategic plan, your organization delivers better results for the employee, the bottom line and your goals.[15] In high-performance organizations, an employee's objectives are aligned with those of the organization. Zeynep Ton has also written about this in *The Good Jobs Strategy: How the Smartest Companies Invest in Employees to Lower Costs and Boost Profits*. Ton finds that investing in your people pays off in performance. In fact, companies that try to reduce labor costs with lower salaries or fewer staff actually cost themselves more

---

[14] Victor Tan, "Benefits of Corporate Culture," *New Straits Times*, July 20, 2002.
[15] Daniel H. Pink, *Drive: The Surprising Truth about What Motivates Us* (New York: Riverhead Books, 2011).

through declining productivity and disengagement.[16] By building this kind of high-performance culture, companies can execute their strategy cost-effectively while improving employee satisfaction and creating a healthy, happy place to work.

High-performance organizational cultures with healthy work environments avoid costs related to stress and high-pressure workplaces. A high-pressure work culture may produce short-term results, but this culture takes a toll on staff over the longer term, leading to turnover, burnout and disengagement. Costs related to health care at high-pressure companies are almost 50% higher than at lower-pressure organizations. The American Psychological Association has estimated that 550 million working days are lost each year due to stress, the same reason for 60% to 90% of visits to doctors, according to research cited by the American Institute of Stress Institute.[17] What really motivates and supports healthy employees is a supportive corporate environment and the opportunity to add value.

ii) Teamwork

The most successful organizations have tremendously strong teams. While some executives might pick favorites and over-rely on individuals who stand out in meetings, the most successful groups are those who row together, with each member of the team contributing to the same goal. In the words of Red Hat CEO James Whitehurst who in June 2015, published a book with Harvard Business Review Press entitled "The Open Organization: Igniting Passion and Performance" showing how open principles of management—based on transparency, participation, and community—can help organizations navigate and succeed in a fast-paced connected era. "Business problems today are too big for any one person to solve. Agile teams are

---

[16] Zeynep Ton, *The Good Jobs Strategy: How the Smartest Companies Invest in Employees to Lower Costs and Boost Profits ("New York: Houghton Mifflin" 2014).*
[17] Emma Seppälä and Kim Cameron, "Proof That Positive Work Cultures Are More Productive," *Harvard Business Review,* Dec. 1, 2015 (accessed March 10, 2017). Available at https://hbr.org/2015/12/proof-that-positive-work-cultures-are-more-productive.

much more effective at solving problems than are lone genius-
es."

A big part – indeed, a benefit – of building a strong execution
culture is the development of an exceptionally strong team.
With the same goal in plain view for all employees, there is no
room for show-offs who compete with colleagues for attention
from the boss.[18] Instead, build an organization where everyone
is investing in each other's success. As we describe later,
aligned, goal-oriented teams are one of the seven key elements
of a high-performance, constructive culture. In this environment, employees are encouraged to be creative. While working
in groups, they welcome their responsibilities, make decisions
independently and hold colleagues and leaders accountable.
There is ownership in their work, leading to a higher level of
commitment and loyalty. Ann Barnes tells says the one think
that could be missing from the traditional planning process that
could cause lack of commitment is engaging the emotions and
beliefs of the team. "I think the planning process is a logical,
formal business approach which is a strong mental exercise but
doesn't include the emotions and beliefs of the team". Then
while evaluating options we ask questions like:

> Which options make the most sense financially? Which op-
> tions will drive the greater success long term? Which
> options align with our vision? Very rarely do we ask, Which
> options can you feel? Which options feel like they can be-
> come part of who we are?

"I think if we can refocus the group from pure logic and include the emotional pieces of driving strategy more teams will
find success". [19]

This kind of teamwork is both a fundamental element of strategy execution and a gratifying workplace benefit you can be
proud of. You will run a better organization with more engaged
employees whose goals do not prioritize their own career ad-

---

[18] Emma Seppälä and Kim Cameron, "Proof That Positive Work Cultures Are More
Productive."
[19] Ann Barnes President and CEO MedData, interview with authors (October 2017)

vancement. Have you ever heard the anecdote about President John F. Kennedy's visit to the NASA space center? While unverified, the timeless anecdote is illustrative. Kennedy was touring the center during the 1960s space race. Noticing a janitor doing some work, he approached the man to introduce himself. He asked what the janitor was doing. "Well, Mr. President," the man responded, "I'm helping put a man on the moon."

In an ideal team culture, each team member feels accountable for goals. They feel they have permission to bring forward innovative solutions, whether it's about frontline software issues or executives' discussion of strategy. Team leaders, from executives to group managers, show the way by example. They take responsibility for their actions and foster open, honest communications by practicing it themselves. Employees feel empowered and recognize the high priorities of teamwork and knowledge-sharing. This kind of teamwork is the opposite of a culture where employees do as they're told, feel they must not rock the boat and do whatever it takes to please managers. Your employees are smart and have a lot to contribute. Allow them to thrive while getting the most out of their enterprise and capabilities.

iii) Goal Attainment

Do you ever feel like your weeks are overtaken by a need to respond to urgent demands, that you can't stay focused on your strategy? We've all been there. It's what Chris McChesney, Jim Huling and Sean Covey, authors of *The 4 Disciplines of Execution*, call being caught up in the day-to-day "whirlwind" of work.[20] There's just too much to do. But strategy execution is about staying focused. When you're focused, you're acting on the most important objectives. Before you know it, you're achieving your goals. It's one of the most important reasons to care about developing a high-performance culture. What is an

[20] Chris McChesney, Sean Covey and Jim Huling, *The 4 Disciplines of Execution: Achieving Your Wildly Important Goals* (New York: Franklin Covey Co., 2012).

organization that can't reach its goals? Organizations exist to aspire to and reach desired outcomes. If they can't be attained consistently, the organization will not reach its potential and may possibly fail.

Louis Gerstner Jr., former CEO of IBM Corporation, learned how important culture was in the 1990s when he took on the unenviable challenge of turning around the company, making it solvent and transitioning it to viability. Early on, Gerstner saw that IBM's biggest challenge was its culture. He had to transform the company from a culture of decentralization and relentless, individualistic salespeople to one of teamwork. He needed employees to shift away from individual product pricing and protecting their own turf toward sharing technical plans and creating common standards. Gerstner used new ways to measure results and provided rewards for teamwork. He instilled a belief in team members that they needed to compete with IBM's rivals – not internally with their own sales colleagues. How did he change these attitudes and behaviors? Beneath the company's processes and organizational climate, he found there remained. A sense of values and identity that could be reclaimed and nurtured. He found that, using these basic values, the culture could be rebuilt, reshaped and renewed. "It took me to age 55 to figure that out. I always viewed culture as one of those things you talked about, like marketing and advertising. It was one of the tools that a manager had at his or her disposal when you think about an enterprise. The thing I have learned at IBM is that culture is everything," Gerstner recalled.[21]

Every leader and executive wants to build an organization that can more successfully reach its goals. As Gerstner found, communication, rewards and measurement were key to changing the culture and improving results. In the coming chapters,

---

[21] Martha Lagace, "Gerstner: Changing Culture at IBM - Lou Gerstner Discusses Changing the Culture at IBM," *HBS Working Knowledge*, Sept. 12, 2002 (accessed March 20, 2017). Available at http://hbswk.hbs.edu/archive/3209.html; see also Louis V. Gerstner, Jr., *Who Says Elephants Can't Dance? Leading a Great Enterprise through Dramatic Change* (New York: Harper Business, 2002).

we discuss how building strategy execution into the fabric of your organization requires new ways of measuring your organization and its results. We describe how to link that up with your rewards, communication, team-building and models of commitment and accountability. It's all about building and maintaining a high-performance culture.

CHAPTER 3
HOW IT WORKS: HIGH-PERFORMANCE CULTURE FRAMEWORK AND PRINCIPLES

UNDERSTANDING CORPORATE CULTURE

This classic "five monkeys experiment," while lore, illustrates how cultural and behavioral norms can develop without its participants understanding why. Researchers put five monkeys in a room, and in the middle, they place a ladder leading up to a basket of bananas. Each time one of the monkeys goes up the ladder for a banana, the researchers spray the others with water. The monkeys aren't happy about the water so, after a few sprays, when one of the monkeys starts up the ladder, the others stop him, wrestle him to the ground, whooping and gibbering at him. After a while, no monkey dares go up the ladder, even with the bananas waiting at the top.

The researchers then substitute one of the monkeys for one that isn't familiar with the environment. It immediately tries to go up the ladder for a banana, and the others wrestle it down, whooping and gibbering. After a few attempts, the new monkey learns not to go up. A second monkey is substituted, and the process is repeated. Soon, the first substituted monkey is helping to pull the new one down from the ladder. A third and fourth monkey are substituted, with the whooping and gibbering repeated, and finally a fifth one. At this point, the researchers have stopped using the water. What they've ended up with is a group of five monkeys that were never sprayed, yet they continue to prevent each other from climbing the ladder.

An outside monkey walks in, sees this and asks: "Why the heck are you beating each other up for trying to get a banana?" "We don't know," they answer. "It's just how things are done around here."

Groups of people in businesses, government and other organizations are not so different to the "Five Monkey". They are made up of identifiable and affiliated groups of people, each possessing a culture. In fact, it's impossible to not have an organizational culture. The very presence of people guarantees one. Behaviors can become entrenched in patterns, sometimes for no particular reason. Perhaps there was a good reason for the behavior at one time or another, but often behaviors within an organization fall into a holding pattern – even when they work against the group's broader goals. In this chapter, we provide the broad strokes of how a high-performance culture works.

i) Organizations Are Groups of People

What do we mean by *corporate culture*? First, it's important to understand how complex culture is, how sensitive it is to influence and how it evolves over time. Edgar Schein, psychologist and former professor at the MIT Sloan School of Management, has had a huge impact on our understanding of organizational culture through works like *Organizational Culture and Leadership*.[22] His research has advanced the understanding that a company's organizational culture is both reflected in and influenced by everything within that organization, from what people wear to work to how their office is arranged. An organization whose employees swear out loud in the office, wear jeans and hoodies and routinely challenge their superiors clearly has a different culture than one where employees work quietly under close supervision, dress in power suits and ties and never rock the boat. One of these cultures is not necessarily better than the other – but every culture is different and complex.

---

[22] Edgar H. Schein, *Organizational Culture and Leadership*, 4th ed. (San Francisco: Jossey-Bass, 2010).

Often, the differences between one organizational culture and the next aren't as stark as those described above. Cultural differences are commonly measured in degrees and always reflected in behaviors and beliefs, not vision statements. There can be a vast difference between an organization's stated culture and the behaviors it tolerates. A firm might have well-intentioned slogans like "Reach for the impossible" on walls in boardrooms while its teams are falling well short of deadlines and the management has forgotten about the company strategy. In such a case, employees are clearly not reaching for the impossible, let alone their goals. In fact, they're probably complaining to one another about management decisions that don't make sense and a failure to implement action points.

Organizations are made up of groups of people, making them inherently social. Organizations focused on strategy execution must emphasize the strengths of its employees and clearly communicate their roles and responsibilities to them. Organizational culture gives employees tacit permission to demonstrate what they see as the attitudes and values of the organization. It's paramount that they have a clear understanding of what's expected. When an employee enters their place of work, they should know exactly the behaviors expected of them by the organization and the group.

People within an organization make daily, hourly, even minute-by-minute decisions based on what they observe to be the corporate culture. They see what their peers and leaders are doing. Their behaviors are not based on what the executive team would like them to be. It's based on how those around them act and what the culture tolerates. One of the most common reasons for employee behaviors to be at odds with the stated goals, values and vision is that the behaviors of leaders fail to live up to their own principles. Your organizational culture is the pattern of behaviors that shape what employees consider to be appropriate. It is the foundation of the organization's capacity for change and the speed and efficiency with which things get done. It has everything to do with your will to execute.

ii) Principles of Corporate Culture

Abstract as culture may seem, there are very concrete ways to understand it. Once leaders understand it, they can move toward influencing and developing it. Consider these fundamental principles when thinking about execution and your organizational culture.

1) It is impossible not to have an organizational culture. The presence of people guarantees one.

2) Everyone owns culture, but leaders have the greatest impact on it.

3) Leaders must own and actively manage their organizational culture.

4) Culture usually trumps competency when it comes to results.

5) If you are not getting the results you want, you, as an organization, may not be who you think you are.

There is no single "correct" or highest-performing organizational culture. There are ideal cultures suited to different types of organizations and their goals. A free-form culture with a flat organizational structure, for instance, may work for creative endeavors such as an animation studio. A stricter, hierarchical culture may work better for an industry such as automotive production, where the company must minimize failure rates and manufacturing variability. The right culture for your group will depend on the type of organization. What's important to note is that all business, nonprofit and government enterprises are comprised of identifiable, affiliated groups of people; their behaviors and beliefs are unique and not fixed.

WHAT STRATEGY EXECUTION LOOKS LIKE

We've described what an organization looks like when it's not executing, when it can't deliver. Its goals, strategic plan, vision and leadership are not aligned with its behaviors and culture.

To help you understand how strategy execution works, let's examine what a corporate culture looks like when everything is aligned and performing at a high level. The organization has a strategic plan and processes in place and is delivering on goals.

i) Leaders Within

High-performance cultures activate every employee's "leader within." Every employee embodies more than one kind of leader. There is the person with a title, the working professional who we call the "external leader." This leader is the trained professional who on paper has the skills, knowledge and competencies that the company needs. Second, there is the person without a title, who we call the "leader within." This leader is a professional 24-7, the person within who motivates and counsels themselves to activate – or not activate – what they know.

Let's take Sherri, an executive assistant on a project team. She receives a complaint from a client who says the project is being held up by a technical problem and is at risk of not proceeding as it should. Sherri has a possible solution that she believes will satisfy the client, but there is no one available for the rest of the day to approve the action. Her external leader knows what to do and how to perform the task at hand. But what does her leader within say? It could say: "Don't bother. Each time you've had a suggestion, you've been told by your leader and colleagues, 'Don't try that; it won't work.' So don't offer anything." Or does her leader within instead counsel: "We are at a critical point in the project and I truly believe this will make a difference." In a high-performance culture, the organization's expected behaviors encourage employees to use their leaders within to make independent judgment calls and decisions. They counsel themselves toward positive, constructive actions.

The world around our desks has the greatest impact on our expectations and behaviors. It's the little dilemmas like Sherri's that make the difference in strategy execution. The decisions of just one individual can spread rapidly, having an exponential effect as they propagate throughout the group. We make tens of thousands of decisions per day, our leaders within advising us frequently. Multiply, say, fifteen thousand decisions per day by the number of people in your organization for an idea of who is responsible for strategy execution. If even a fraction of the people in an organization suppress their leader within, figuratively pulling the bedcovers over their heads for the day, their commitment is removed. Such a pattern sends an organization's performance numbers into an alarmingly suboptimal range. On the other hand, if leaders counsel employees that their best contributions will be accepted, that they are making a difference in the organization and helping to attain goals, there are outwardly positive ripple effects on engagement and results.

What is it that pushes employees to activate what they know? What influences their choices at critical junctures day-to-day, pushing your organization's performance into execution mode? Largely, it is what people hear and see in the course of their workday that offers them the most definitive cues about how to behave, fit in and be successful.

ii) Behavioral Styles

Over 30 years ago, psychologist Dr. Clayton Lafferty developed an important tool, called the Circumplex, to categorize and measure organizational culture. Since then, thanks to ongoing research by Dr. Robert Cooke of Human Synergistics International as well as work by other organizations using the tool around the world, the Circumplex has been providing quantitative insight into what and who drives organizational performance. Various diagnostic instruments based on the Circumplex can uncover the nature of an organization's culture and the type of behaviors and beliefs dominating it.

The Circumplex finds three broad behavioral styles underlying an organization's performance: constructive, passive (defensive) and aggressive (defensive). These help leaders understand what is happening within an organization and provide specific recommendations for transforming and improving its culture to achieve results.

The two defensive styles, passive and aggressive, are not aligned with execution. Passive styles of behavior are related to disempowerment, disengagement, following orders and other behaviors that don't rock the boat. Aggressive styles are related to resisting change, growing and defending one's power base, taking punitive measures against others and internal competition. The constructive style in the Circumplex, on the other hand, is most aligned with execution. These are behaviors related to focusing on goal achievement, taking personal ownership over tasks, accountability, positive conflict resolution, talent attraction and retention, and teamwork and mentoring. These constructive behaviors are those that organizations want to shape, nurture and develop as they work toward an ideal high-performance culture.

There are substantial differences between the defensive and constructive styles of behavior. Human Synergistics and ACHIEVEBLUE Corporation have found that the best-performing cultures are dominated by constructive styles. In the same vein, these dominant constructive behaviors are powerful, keeping in check the emergence of aggressive, passive and defensive cultures. Organizations with these constructive cultures effectively encourage people to step up to suppress defensive behaviors like internal competition, confrontation and focusing on flaws. High-performance cultures have fewer oppositional or power characteristics like demands for loyalty and outperforming one's peers at the expense of the team. While defensive behaviors may be functional in moderation, in excess they run counter to performance and can significantly reduce your productivity and diminish results. For strategy execution, organizations want a constructive culture of engaged employees, team members who are all rowing together to reach goals.

iii) Constructive Culture, Constructive Feedback

Your organization has a strong constructive culture and is executing its strategy. What does that look like? We've talked about some positive attributes of a high-performance culture, such as employee engagement, positive values and teamwork. But a constructive culture also requires alignment with your organizational climate, with the right processes, programs and systems in place to support it. Cultures that execute effectively have clear roles for employees and accessible channels and systems that encourage accountability and steady, clear communications.

One of the most important things we repeatedly hear from executives is an earnest wish to hear new ideas from their employees. Leaders have expended a great deal of time, energy and money to locate the right hire – that is, someone whose cache of expertise and experience brings a competitive advantage. But far too many companies don't get the most out of their team members. Employees can put in face time and complete tasks, but what about their brightest ideas for change? Healthy communication, and hearing from your team members, is one of the great attributes of a high-performance culture.

Let's say your organization is strong in constructive styles of behaviors and calls a group meeting with executives present. Will employees' leaders challenge their managers on proposals that don't make sense, that aren't in line with the strategy? Will they present their best ideas? Absolutely. Consider the same meeting in an organization whose cultural style is defensive. Will employees present their most innovative ideas? Not likely. Rather than orienting the meeting toward strategic visioning, forward-thinking planning or cross-functional conversations involving other departments, they will simply provide updates. They are doing their jobs with little or no innovation.

In constructive cultures, employees have a clear idea of their roles and responsibilities. Employees who understand their role and how they can contribute take ownership of their tasks within the organization, as well as in its overall success. They are committed. Employees openly talk not only about strategy but also about the organization's culture; indeed, the culture is understood and embraced by the entire organization and is seen as vital to its success. When every employee knows what the organization and the culture expect of them, accountability follows. Success or failure is easy to understand, reward and correct when responsibilities and expectations are clearly communicated and agreed upon.

What are some signs you're leading a constructive high-performance culture? Well, are employees concerned about working together to lead the organization toward goal achievement? Does the CEO walk the talk and have an open-door culture that encourages employees' questions, doubts and new ideas? Do all members of the organization feel personal ownership and influence within the organization? If the answers are yes, you're probably already there. If the answers are no, there's probably a need to shift from a short-term focus on results to building an organization that's energized and delivering results, year after year.

CHAPTER 4
THE SEVEN ELEMENTS OF STRATEGY EXECUTION: CLARITY

You can't execute your strategy without the seven elements, and we start with clarity for a reason. Communicating with your employees so that they see and understand clearly may be the single most important element of execution. Excellent communication is clarity; clarity is clear seeing. To create and sustain a high-performance organization, the first step is defining your goals with transparency and precision. Your goals and outcomes should be strong enough that you can measure them within degrees of achievement. The new strategic plan and its intended goals must be well-defined, sensible and communicated so that everyone in the organization has an understanding of their roles, tasks and purpose. Everyone within the organization, no matter their position, must possess clear seeing: an understanding of the goals, challenges and rewards ahead of themselves and the entire group. They must feel and see that the objectives they are working toward are shared. They understand what their contribution is and what the end product or service looks like. Their vision of the path ahead is as certain as that of the executives and leaders. Every employee should be able to answer this simple question: How does this new strategy benefit me?

i) Alignment of Vision, Values, Strategy and Outcomes

The first step in effectively communicating your strategy is ensuring consistency in your communication. This means consistency in everything your organization does. Communication is not simply words and text. Actions and behaviors communicate as much as what leaders say. Consistency in communication is what we call aligning your strategy, or cascading it, throughout the organization, so that what the organization espouses is aligned with everything it does and everything its people do. All things, from values to incentives, point to the same vision and strategic plan. Too many companies and organizations develop a great strategy and present it with fanfare and support. Its people proceed to go back to their day jobs while the company fails to align processes, resources and front-end activities with the new plan. Strategy can't be executed at the executive level. It must be cascaded throughout the organization so that teams are not operating in silos. Your principles, metrics and goals are positioned the same way as your employees' behaviors: The culture, strategy and all of your communications are aligned.

In the early days, before shoe company Zappos.com was purchased by Amazon for US $1.2 billion, its CEO Tony Hsieh decided the retailer needed a transformation. He set out to shape an ideal culture aligned with the goal of providing superior customer service. He aligned the business, including employee rewards, with customer service. Employees, seeing the strategy clearly and feeling invested in it, bought in. The corporate culture became so focused on the new objective that sales reps went as far as sending customers to competitors when Zappos was out of stock in a specific shoe size. With a strategic focus on the customer, everyone, including vendors, knew what the company was all about. Employees became more engaged and passionate about their work, and outcomes followed. From the start of the transformation in 2003 to the end of 2004, revenues surged by 600%. Says Hsieh: "Your culture is your brand. Customer service shouldn't just be a department, it should be the entire company."[23]

---

[23] Brian Solis, "Zappos' Tony Hsieh Delivers Happiness Through Service and Innovation," BrianSolis.com, April 11, 2011 (accessed April 12, 2017). Available at www.briansolis.com/2011/04/zappos-tony-hsieh-happiness.

Alignment does not exist as a theory for your organization. It must be practiced. It's not enough for the slogans on your website to be aligned with your corporate ethics rules. Your compensation incentives must also be aligned with one common strategic goal shared by everyone. The most difficult part of aligning your organization is probably the responsibility of listening to your people. You need to understand their needs, motivations and any technical challenges so that you can empower them and align their behaviors with the strategy and goals. Alignment is also important in attracting the talent you want. Today, companies are hiring from a much more astute, younger generation that has little tolerance for hypocrisy. Millennials and the Gen Z generation do not have patience for misaligned values. Gen Z, a powerful group of consumers and the world's future leaders, is considered the most socially aware generation yet. More than previous generations, they research brands before buying them and discuss companies and their values on social media.[24]

Younger generations are paying closer attention and organizations are under more pressure to embrace higher moral standards. It's more important than ever for organizations to be aligned. Organizations can't get away with hypocrisies like having a public-facing vision and set of values that contradict what's practiced internally. Already, rising global transparency and the corporate experience with social media suggest companies can no longer focus on profit margin above all else. Higher standards of accountability are becoming the norm. Philosopher Daniel Dennett theorizes that quickening rates of transparency, due to digital technologies and platforms, will eventually make it nearly impossible to keep secrets. Organizations' "information membranes" no longer serve as a protective

---

[24] Cynthia Johnson, "Generation Z and the Future of Business," *Entrepreneur*, March 3, 2017 (accessed April 22, 2017). Available at www.entrepreneur.com/article/289847.

barrier, a trend that he says puts major institutions in jeopardy – even banks, large corporations, government and the courts.[25]

Obviously, we don't want to suggest that the future of the courts is in question. But it's time to know what your organization stands for and to make sure it's practiced inside and out. Executives who fail to align their behaviors with their vision, values and strategy will fail in the execution part. Support will fall away from the people you need most – the people who execute the plan. Organizations whose actions and decisions are not aligned with the culture and the strategy lose credibility with their people, not to mention their clients. Your people can see misalignment, which fosters cynicism and dysfunction. Where management doesn't walk the talk, new initiatives stall. Worse, they are quietly laughed at by team members and frontline staff. Misalignment as seemingly small as having the wrong systems in place – perhaps the wrong technology, which hampers employees' efforts to advance the plan – can foster an environment and behaviors that work against your goals. Alignment, on the other hand, is powerful. Team members, rather than gossiping with colleagues about another hypocritical decision, tell each other: "This organization has really figured this thing out" or "I appreciate all the updates explaining to us why we're doing this." It's the difference between engagement and disengagement and, in the end, losses and gains.

ii) KUBA Communication

We encourage leaders to use the KUBA model for communication. KUBA, a way to translate knowledge into action, stands for Know, Understand, Believe and Act. It is a way to manage clarity. When team members can see clearly and fully understand why they're doing what they're doing, they can put their beliefs into action.

---

[25] https://www.ft.com/content/96187a7a-fce5-11e6-96f8-3700c5664d30 Philosopher Daniel Dennett on AI, robots and religion

- **Know.** Good communication starts with employees knowing what's expected of them – the particular ways they are expected to act and behave. At all times, your people need to know what will be happening, who will be doing what, when it's happening and any changes in plan or direction.

- **Understand.** The why of the plan is critical. Your people need to understand why their actions and behaviors are important. In addition to the why, explain how their actions and the plan will impact them, how they will support it and what will be expected of them. Employees must understand the why of any changes to the plan or actions, or the causes of any setbacks, along the way. This means involving employees directly in problem-resolution, problem-solving, new directions and changes in general. Involving them in the process and ensuring understanding gains employee commitment.

- **Believe.** Knowing and understanding deliver belief. Employees need to believe in the change and the plan for themselves. To gain their commitment, they must believe change is necessary and well thought out. Belief is critical to high-performance organizations – it advances the strategic plan.

- **Act.** When employees know, understand and believe in the plan and any changes to it, they act on their beliefs. Action backed by belief is powerful; it is employee engagement defined. Your people will act and behave in ways that support the change, advance the strategy and align with expectations.

Effective communication using the KUBA model changes a team member's thought process, from skeptical questioning to belief and action. For instance, one team member's thought process may shift this way: I'm skeptical of all this change. What's happening? How does it affect me? Where can I learn more? Changing makes sense. How can I convince others?

Let's say a company that sells software is experiencing off-target sales. They're not growing in line with the strategic plan, and the sales reps are not seen frequently in the office. Other team members working on the technology side start to gossip that the sales team is not doing their fair share. Where are they all the time? What are they doing? This company faces both a practical problem (why are sales not growing) and a communication problem (misunderstanding). For the most part, the teams know what's expected of them. But here, they don't really know what's happening. The communication is breaking down when it comes to knowing who's doing what and why. They need to know that the sales team is having great difficulty with the product because the competitor's upgraded version is slightly cheaper. Leaders must communicate this to all teams – plus the fact that the sales reps are facing steady rejections and, under significant pressure to deliver on their targets, they're pounding the pavement for additional client meetings. On top of that, they're withdrawing amid very high stress levels.

Through communication, all teams in this scenario will come to understand the situation. They'll feel the same burden as their fellow sales reps as they learn the effects of the sales problem on job satisfaction and rewards. They'll start to learn that the sales reps are in fact fearing for their jobs when they have a bad sales day, that they feel like they're not part of the organization.

As departments communicate what they know, management starts to receive reports about what clients are saying about the software. Now both management and other teams understand why the sales reps were acting the way they were. They also understand why they need to make a change to the product – and introduce its new version with a pricing strategy. This understanding about the change gives all teams the strength to believe. They believe in themselves and the support they have around them. All team members come together and communicate about the issue at hand and the change going forward. Leaders want everyone to know and feel that everyone is in this together, that they are all responsible for the company's revenues and profits. Employees appreciate and respect the efforts of colleagues. When employees believe, they act. Acting does not only mean executing. It also means further knowing and understanding – and sharing their ups and downs with each other on a daily basis. Recognizing the broader team goal, team members have respect for what's asked of them, no matter where the request comes from. They act as one team. They believe that the strategy works and that they are supported by a team who also believes.

Leaders can't skip a step in the KUBA model. Each block – Know, Understand, Believe and Act – builds on the preceding one. Act, or the execution part, can't happen without team members knowing, understanding and believing. Leaders who attempt to move their teams directly from knowing to acting may find they get compliance – but commitment won't follow.

iii) Aligned Communication

Without clear and constant communication, employees tend to diverge from their expected tasks, responsibilities and behaviors, disrupting performance. Communication has many forms and does not just include language. Communication is leading by example, and, important, listening. Leaders need a clear message aligned with their values and the strategy, and they must stick to it.

A CLEAR STRATEGY

Language is important. What is the language of your culture, and how will you communicate it? Imagine how ineffective it would be to hand a new employee a three-ring binder containing pages of information about "values." Corporate culture isn't transmitted through binders. Language must be aligned with your values and strategy, and all leaders must have a clear understanding of the kind of language they are to use. Information can be relayed through your tone, diction, body language and even the clothing worn at the office. Details matter to the people on the ground floor executing the strategy. They will see right away when language and behaviors aren't aligned with what's coming from the top. Are leaders "walking the talk"?

Strong leaders do so much. They must not only see the future, have a vision and create a strategy for it, they must also communicate objectives in a way that ensures everyone, from vice presidents to frontline staff, understands the goals ahead of them. As discussed in the KUBA communication model, employees too often do not know why they're doing what they're doing, sometimes with disastrous consequences. Why does a worker in an animal feed production facility need to thoroughly clean the vats between different feed productions? Because chicken feed is poisonous to horses. One worker in such a facility in New Jersey, who wasn't told why he needed to clean the vats, took a shortcut, failing to clean them. As a result, several horses died.[26] The lesson is that employees across your organization must understand the why of your strategy. The message about the strategy must be cascaded from the office of the president to team leaders, who are coached about how to communicate it to team members. What's in it for them? What does the end product look like? How do we get there? Why are we doing this? On an individual level, every employee needs to understand the strategy. It's clear communication that will get you there.

FROM THE OUTSET

New employees should have a clear picture of the strategy, the culture and what's expected of them from the very outset. By this we mean the *very outset*. Even a job interview should communicate expectations at a high level. From there, thoughtful training for new hires instills the culture. Your training program for new employees has a major effect on how they

---

[26] Paul L. Marciano, *Carrots and Sticks Don't Work: Building a Culture of Employee Engagement with the R.E.S.P.E.C.T. Principle* (New York: McGraw-Hill, 2010), 152.

view and adopt the culture. It truly is their introduction to the company and what is expected of them going forward.

Communicating your culture to a new team member is both active (what they learn through training materials and instruction) and passive (what they learn through socialization and the behaviors of those around them). Training programs should not only clearly communicate the strategy, but they should also be designed to communicate the culture in both active and passive ways. Employees should come away with an understanding of the culture and enthusiasm for and knowledge about the strategy. They should understand their position and responsibilities and the why of their tasks, regardless of their "rank" within the organization. You don't want new employees who, unfamiliar with the culture, unintentionally start to disrupt its beliefs, standards and customs.

Sleep Country Canada is known for maintaining a strong training program that supports its execution. Its strategy is to deliver superior customer service, and it is embedded into the beliefs of the company. For instance, the company offers a professional mattress delivery service, complete with installation, removal of the old mattress and a cleanup of any packaging. New hires on the front lines – the people executing strategy – are immediately put into an extensive six-week training program. They learn about products, sales and customer service. Right off the bat, employees learn the culture and values of trust, professionalism, friendliness and customer satisfaction. They meet leaders in the firm, establishing multiple points of contact inside management. Before employees even start dealing with customers, they are given a clear line of sight on their objectives, the culture and the company mission.

Stephen Gunn, executive co-chairman and co-founder of the company, says new hires are usually surprised by the initial training. "The most common feedback I get, and it's almost universal, is, 'Wow. No one's ever done this for me before,'" he says. The training program teaches new hires that the people investing in them want them to succeed, and that as they grow, they are expected to help others succeed. After their training, as new Sleep Country employees head to work on location for the first time, Gunn tells them:

> "One thing I want you to remember is what it feels like to be brand-new here. I want you to appreciate how much everyone is trying to help you because, before you know it, you'll be on the other side and you'll have a rookie standing next to you, and I don't want to hear that you're acting like some big shot know-it-all. It's your responsibility to be as helpful to the newcomer standing next to you as people were to you." That message, done from Day 1, consistently for the last 20 years across the company, has fostered an ethic and a culture.[27]

From the very outset, the strategy, the culture – and what's expected – is communicated and reinforced.

FOCUS, REPEAT

Imagine a bank CEO executing a merger strategy. The new strategy for the company is to grow with the acquisition and adopt the superior retail services of the acquired bank. It's a huge undertaking, and it involves changing the habits and behaviors of thousands of staff. Ed Clark, former chairman and chief executive officer of Canada Trust, confronted this challenge, becoming chief executive of the bank as it merged with TD Bank Group. Clark is an excellent communicator and, with a clear communication strategy, he traveled across the country to TD divisions, giving speeches to keep employees focused on core principles like excellent customer service and the streamlining of processes.[28]

What was interesting about the speeches was their consistent message. Recalls Robert MacLellan, then an executive at TD who went on the road with Clark:

---

[27] Stephen Gunn, Sleep Country Canada, interview with the authors (December 2014).
[28] Robert MacLellan, former TD executive, interview with the authors (March 2016).

He gave the same speech every year. Every single year, the same speech. I said to him: "Why are you doing that? Don't you think you sound silly, giving the same speech?" He said: "You know, Rob, people really like to hear the same thing over and over because it makes them comfortable. Here we are in the middle of doing all of this change and they just want to know that I haven't changed, that I still have the same vision, and what they're doing is the right thing. They just need to keep doing it. [29]"

Clark's communication was clear, consistent and simple. He was driving home the new strategy, helping to cascade it throughout the organization. He kept employees focused on a few key principles, and worked to "just hammer them and hammer them and hammer them – totally focused," MacLellan says. "Strategy execution is really hard," he adds. "It sounds like it should be easy, but it's so easy to get distracted. It's so important to remind people where it is they're going, why it's important to go there and what the end result is going to be, what their role is and how crucial their role is in all of this.[30]"

Communicating a strategy requires focus. It is emphasizing concise, simple and focused messages at both individual and group levels. Rather than listing 12 principles for your employees, aim for just a few. A well-articulated message, tailored to teams or individuals where necessary, guides them toward a common goal. Try over communicating at first to get a feel for it. Chris Nickerson, senior vice president of sales distribution and marketing at NEI Investments, says he doesn't believe there is such a thing as over communication. "Constantly communicate 'Here is our strategy, here are the tactics,'" he says. Team members should feel empowered by your communications. The strategy should be so clear that they can see when there's divergence from it. Nickerson says: "Everything we do as an organization needs to revolve around these tactics

[29] Robert MacLellan, former TD executive, interview with the authors (March 2016).
[30] Robert MacLellan, former TD executive, interview with the authors (March 2016).

in order to achieve this strategy." Empower people to say 'That's not part of our tactical map," because if they're empowered to say that, then we can recognize "Oh, we're going off on a tangent."[31] People want to feel they are making a contribution. Reassure them their actions have an impact.

Internal corporate communications often lack ambition and feeling. According to David Hopkinson, chief commercial officer at Maple Leaf Sports & Entertainment, leaders need to select corporate objectives that resonate with their team members. This means choosing more ambitious goals that require collective team efforts to meet. A bank CEO telling employees they're going to post the best three quarters the bank has ever seen doesn't cut it. What objectives will motivate your people? For Hopkinson, what's worked is: "What we're trying to do is build the world's finest sports entertainment company, and we're trying to win championships. You're either in, or you're in the way," he says. That's the kind of thing employees want to hear consistently.[32]

Pay attention to tone. It's consequential because employees pick up on it. They feel it. Tone, and conveying the emotion behind your words, can go a long way to connecting with staff. Communicating honestly and what you feel tends to simplify the message and make it more memorable. Adds Hopkinson: "People have trouble putting their feelings into words and having words put into their feelings. We're all wrapped up in our own lives, and our own lives are busy. [It goes back to] the simplicity of communication. [33]"

---

[31] Chris Nickerson, senior vice president, sales and, NEI Investments, interview with the authors (October 2016).

[32] David Hopkinson, chief commercial officer, Maple Leaf Sports & Entertainment, interview with the authors (December 2014).

[33] David Hopkinson, chief commercial officer, Maple Leaf Sports & Entertainment, interview with the authors (December 2014).

LISTEN

Keeping your people focused and engaged is not just a matter of town halls, corporate newsletters and speeches. Leaders must know how to communicate both big-tent messages to the entire organization as well as detailed messages to small groups and individuals. Cascaded throughout, all of these communications must be aligned with the strategy. Two-way dialogue, for the receiving and sharing of ideas and constructive feedback, ensures the strategy is common and understood among all employees. Messaging, while aligned with the strategy, can be tailored to the needs of the group or individuals at hand. This is done through listening, problem-solving and adapting the message. What are middle managers and frontline staff saying about your strategy? What are the hundreds of questions and problems confronting them that leaders never anticipated?

A bank with two thousand branches, for instance, needs the customer to have the same experience at every branch. Frontline staff need a very clear understanding of their roles and the culture and strategy they're advancing. The frontline staff need focus and guidance, while the leaders need staff buy-in to the plan. Listening – and responding with clear communication about the way forward – goes a long way to creating buy-in. Communication, while aligned with the strategy, must be adapted to the group and individual levels to keep frontline and back-office employees focused, engaged and motivated. "If you don't have them, you can never win the customer," says MacLellan, recalling the importance of frontline branch staff in a big bank. "If your employees turn against you at the branch level, that will become apparent to the customers. They will sense that, and negative things will happen from that. [34]"

For effective two-way communication, leaders should be accessible. Hopkinson has taken a page from Daniel H. Pink's

---

[34] Robert MacLellan, former TD executive, interview with the authors (March 2016).

book *Drive: The Surprising Truth about What Motivates Us*, in which the author suggests that executives hold office hours.[35] Hopkinson says he schedules office hours – even though he doesn't have time for them – because they are so valuable. He allots two hours per week during which staff can book 15-minute sessions, bringing their questions, concerns, suggestions or comments. Topics raised tend to range from career advancement to problems faced by employees. For complainers, he asks them to propose a solution. "I don't think there's any one thing I do that gives me greater credibility with the team here than being that open and accessible," Hopkinson says. "It has been an unbelievable connector organizationally, just to be able to establish that reputation." [36]

BRAND CONSISTENCY

It's important to prevent inconsistencies from developing within your brand or between your internal and external brand. All communications should be aligned with your values and strategy. That means all language should reflect a highly constructive culture focused on goals. Ensure that your principles, values and marketing materials are consistent and include them in your annual communications plans or action items. Internally, identify your values and principles repeatedly in communications about the strategy.

Communications materials may include monthly newsletters from the office of the president or the executive who is sponsoring the strategy. The package may offer important quotes and a story aligned with the strategy and values, perhaps an anecdote about an employee in the organization who is "living" the organization's constructive culture. Social media is also an effective tool for promoting and harmonizing the brand. As the organization develops a high-performance culture, encourage

---

[35] Daniel H. Pink, *Drive: The Surprising Truth about What Motivates Us* (New York: Riverhead Books, 2009).
[36] Daniel H. Pink, *Drive: The Surprising Truth about What Motivates Us* (New York: Riverhead Books, 2009).

team members and colleagues to post positive messages about their workplaces on Facebook and Instagram. Facebook pages for teams can serve as constructive forums where colleagues may highlight their activities, events and charitable work – which further motivates team members. As your brand succeeds internally, colleagues can promote it externally, ensuring it's consistent with both employees and customers.

CHAPTER 5
THE SEVEN ELEMENTS OF STRATEGY EXECUTION: COMMITMENT

A high-performance culture establishes behavioral norms where team members come to work every day with commitment, drive and focus. The right tools and incentives – from constructive rewards to building trust and team attitudes – further that commitment and drive. Managers need to understand the high level of commitment that's necessary to embark on and execute a new strategic plan. They must recognize it will probably involve much more effort, planning, detail and personnel management than they had ever expected. The strategic plan must be understood by everyone, from top to bottom. For those at the top, a prime responsibility is ensuring those at the bottom are as committed as they are.

i) Rewards and Compensation

Think carefully about your rewards. Are they set up to incent the same behaviors you want your culture to have? Are they encouraging behaviors that align with your goals? Is your strategy cascaded into your rewards? It's very important to recognize that rewards drive actions – sometimes unintended actions that can push your culture off course. Consider the call center manager who communicates the strategic objective of superior customer service. But he then establishes rewards for reps based on the number of calls they field per day. He is in for a surprise. The establishment of this reward system sends customer satisfaction ratings downward as the representatives forget customer service – they're focused on getting to the next call as quickly as possible. It's an example of rewarding actions that are not aligned with the strategy of superior customer service. If the company's objective is excellent customer service, that's what should be measured and rewarded. Instead, customer satisfaction ratings could be provided to the call center employees, and those who receive a string of high ratings could be rewarded.

Rewards and compensation are linked back to the importance of excellent communication. Using rewards to reinforce behavior is a matter of understanding what motivates your people and ensuring the rewards are aligned. For the former, managers and team leaders need to know their people on an individual basis. They need to understand what makes them tick, what drives them. Once they do, they need to explain how the new strategy is going to be great for that individual – and that's where the rewards come in. One person may be highly motivated by a reward for which another team member feels indifferent. For instance, there can be big differences within multigenerational teams. A team member over the age of 50 may be thinking about retirement savings while a millennial may be thinking about work-life balance and spending time with their young children.

Says Chris Nickerson of NEI:

> Compensation drives behavior. Compensation is different for me, different for you, different for the next person. You might value a day off more than cash. You might value a pat on the back and a gift card more than a day off and cash.... It's all about the understanding what is important for person. If you're trying to use compensation to change behavior, then build it so that it changes behavior.... We only make a change that's better for you to ultimately better for us as an organization. We're never going to change targets three-quarters of the way through the year. We're never going to change compensation three-quarters of the way through the year. Everybody's going to know right out of the gate what their potential is to earn. For us, it's all about creating the right culture and that we have a fun place to work. Fun is

extremely important. The respect that we have for our people is overwhelming. What they do on a daily basis is very tough [for] everybody across the organization, but we win together.[37]

Nickerson says one of the most important things he's learned about compensation and rewards is that, since they are meant to drive behaviors, the rewards targets must be within the control of the employee. He recognizes that his salespersons can't control the financial markets or the performance of the company's products. What they can control, however, is their behaviors, their discipline and their team contributions.

While financial rewards can be used to drive behaviors, to drive the right behaviors they must also be aligned with the culture and values. For rewards to contribute to strategy execution, they should be tailored to do two things: (*a*) fit with the interests of the individual working on the team; and (*b*) align with your ideal constructive culture. If your company vision is healthy, happy customers, perhaps a paid day off is a reward that better aligns with your strategy and the interests of the employee. Or perhaps they'd prefer a free, healthy, delicious lunch with a colleague at a restaurant or a vacation with their family to a wellness resort.

Ensure promotions are also aligned with your values and culture. Leaders affect culture by every decision they make, from their selection of business systems and organizational structures to policies and rules. The influence of their decisions also extends to who they promote to what positions and when. Leaders' actions always communicate a story to employees. What is the story you want to communicate? What is being rewarded? Does the leader espouse a collaborative, constructive culture but then promote highly oppositional or competitive people? Misaligned decisions encourage cynicism and behaviors that get in the way of execution.[38] In decisions, always

---

[37] Chris Nickerson, senior vice president, sales distribution and marketing, NEI Investments, interview with the authors (October 2016).
[38] David Hopkinson, chief commercial officer, Maple Leaf Sports & Entertainment, interview with the authors (December 2014).

send a clear message about priorities. They should reflect your culture's collective expectations.

Group rewards can be helpful to drive behaviors in team environments. While individual rewards remain appropriate in many contexts, especially for external employees or contributors, leaders can use group rewards to encourage teamwork and foster a positive, constructive culture. With group rewards, the collective achievement by a team results in rewards for all of its members. There are several variations of group rewards, with flexibility for managers to design reward systems that best align with the strategy and team structure. Michael Schrage, research fellow at the MIT Sloan School's Center for Digital Business, suggests simply that organizations use a fifty-fifty split between teams and individuals, so that compensation, rewards, bonuses and even recognition is given equally to both individuals and teams. "[F]or every executive utterance praising a high-impact individual, there should be an equally emphatic expression of support for a high-achieving team. For every 'above and beyond' award given to a dedicated individual, there better be a comparable honor given to a team that delivered," he writes.[39] The idea is to avoid rewarding individuals if it comes at any cost to the attitudes of the rest of the group. Maintaining the culture and a team dynamic remains the priority.

ii) Passion and Purpose

Author Daniel Pink has written extensively about how companies are more profitable when they give employees more time and support and the independence to make decisions. What these companies are really doing is giving their employees purpose, the number one motivator for your people and their executions.

---

[39] Michael Schrage, "Reward Your Best Teams, Not Just Star Players," *Harvard Business Review*, June 30, 2015 (accessed March 18, 2017). Available at https://hbr.org/2015/06/reward-your-best-teams-not-just-star-players.

Employees want autonomy, an area of expertise and purpose in their work,[40] and they thrive when given it. Pink argues they are driven more by mastering their art and making a useful contribution than they are by financial rewards. Consider the contributions to open-source computer programming, Pink says. People who help improve free open-source platforms are driven by their contributions, their participation and their mastery of coding. He suggests that if financial incentives were offered to open-source contributors, it would diminish their participation. The financial reward would itself change the focus and intentions of open-source contributors. Of salaries and compensation, Pink says in his interview with Katherine Bell:

> One of the best uses of money as a motivator is to pay people enough to take the issue of money off the table, so people aren't focused on money, they're focused on the work. Once you do that, it's really a matter of tapping the things that the science shows lead to enduring performance, particularly for more complex tasks. And that's a sense of autonomy, self-direction, and the desire to get better and better at something that matters, you can call that mastery, and also purpose, that is, doing what we do in the service of something larger than oneself.[41]

While compensation is important, the right compensation is more important. It can be used to turn an employee's focus to the larger task at hand, and there is no value like outstanding performance, especially when it's collective.

Finding an employee's emotional drive may also be described as helping them find and achieve success, and good leaders help team members do this through goal achievement. All employees have goals, even if they can't articulate them or see them clearly. An organization should communicate clearly with staff to establish personal and professional goals aligned with

---

[40] Daniel H. Pink, *Drive: The Surprising Truth about What Motivates Us* (New York: Riverhead Books, 2009).

[41] *Harvard Business Review. Katherine Bell interview with Daniel H. Pink*, Feb. 18, 2010 (accessed Dec. 3, 2016). Available at https://hbr.org/2010/02/what-motivates-us.

the strategy. Motivating your people to execute a new strategic plan is a massive yet detailed process requiring excellent managers at every level. Ann Barnes states: "The one factor that she has observed with that ensures strategy success is Passion! The feeling and believing in a plan that becomes part of the culture, the team, the individual leaders. When leaders internalize a strategy, they drive it to success and let other lesser priorities fall by the wayside. It is a very natural process at that point!" [42] Leaders, through coaching and good communications plans, should be able to sit where the employee is sitting, see the strategic plan through their eyes and explain how it benefits them. They should be passionate about the plan. Perhaps the organization's new strategic direction will help them achieve a financial reward, promotion or time off to spend with their family. Perhaps success is defined as gaining more recognition from peers, working abroad or learning a new language. It is finding that emotional drive that is connected to the strategy and the bigger picture: the personal goal that is bigger than themselves.

Managers and team leaders should possess an ability to see when team members' successes are not met. Often, this shows up as unhappiness, frustration or anxiety in the workplace. Team leaders must be sensitive to the signs. "[W]hen people display positive emotions like anticipation, happiness or relief, they are signaling that they have had a recent success or are confident about their prospects for success," writes Art Markman, professor of psychology and marketing at University of Texas at Austin. "When they display negative emotions like fear, anxiety, sadness, or disappointment, they are revealing that they have had a goal failure, or they anticipate one." Managers should be observant and coached to recognize that these negative emotions are related to obstacles or goal failures. Noticing the feelings of team members provides an opportunity for team leaders to address them and any other issues standing in the way of the employee's success. Engagement is boosted

---

[42] Ann Barnes, President & CEO MedData, interview with the authors (October 2017).

when employees feel their organization supports their entire life, not just their life at work.[43]

iii) Balance Personal and Organizational

We all have busy lives as we try to juggle the pressures of work, relationships, family time, rest, community involvement, physical activity and personal health. For many professionals, it seems work-life balance has been harder to find, and organizations large and small are appropriately recognizing this. Old notions of putting in 7.5 hours of face time per day are no longer practical in our "always on" lifestyles. Connectivity has rewritten the traditional workplace bargain, turning the nine-to-five workday on its head. Today's employees, especially younger generations, have much different expectations about balancing career demands with personal needs. Many organizations now accommodate employees' wishes to work remotely or slip away on a quiet afternoon to run an errand, rest or respond to family needs. Conversely, when there's a crunch in tasks, employees rise to the occasion. These are some of the employee-employer benefits that come with a high-performance culture: trust, loyalty, motivation and commitment.

While employees demand more personal-needs space than before, leaders must be careful not to emphasize people over tasks to the detriment of the culture. There must be a balance. Upsetting this balance by always putting people first can encourage disengagement and a defensive culture that hampers execution. Allowing excessive space for personal needs may lead to team members interacting with each other in "self-protective" ways that guard personal or emotional security. Or it may lead to the reinforcement of expectations that colleagues emphasize the needs of people at the expense of tasks.

---

[43] Art Markman, "Your Employees' Emotions Are Clues to What Motivates Them," *Harvard Business Review*, May 18, 2015 (accessed June 2, 2017). Available at https://hbr.org/2015/05/your-employees-emotions-are-clues-to-what-motivates-them.

Dr. Robert Cooke and Linda Sharkey, executives in organizational and people development, note that putting people's needs first can lead to the withholding of negative, yet vital constructive feedback on a project. Or it can translate into team members choosing to subordinate themselves to rules even when they know their judgment is the better option. Leaders do not want behaviors to develop where employees suppress their judgment and leaders within. Quite the opposite: Rational risk-taking and individual judgment is essential to execution. Leaders must watch for signs of behaviors that promote "approval-oriented, conventional, dependent, and avoidant behaviors throughout the organization," Cooke and Sharkey say. The culture should not approve of defensive behaviors like withdrawing or self-care to the point that they signal an imbalance. [44]

An imbalance can fall the other way, too. Emphasizing tasks over personal needs can similarly lead to a defensive culture. If employees feel their personal needs are not recognized, the organization may very well develop "aggressive disengagement." In this behavioral style, employees forcefully push colleagues into tasks. They reinforce and require team members, both subordinates and peers, to put work and short-term priorities over the needs of individuals. Staff tend to pursue their own objectives, competing instead of collaborating. Their behaviors support oppositional, power-oriented attitudes and beliefs in perfectionism. It is an unhealthy, defensive cultural style that leads to disengagement and lower performance. [45]

Once again, leaders play a critical role here. Defensive cultures tend to be fostered by managers who use more "restrictive" tactics, communicating what's been done wrong. They stress

---

[44] Robert A. Cooke and Linda Sharkey, "Developing Constructive Leader Impact," *Consulting Today,* 2006 (accessed Nov. 13, 2016). Available at www.humansynergistics.com/Files/ResearchAndPublications/Consulting_Today_C ooke_Sharkey_Constructive_Leader_Impact.pdf
[45] Robert A. Cooke and Linda Sharkey, "Developing Constructive Leader Impact," *Consulting Today,* 2006 (accessed Nov. 13, 2016). Available at www.humansynergistics.com/Files/ResearchAndPublications/Consulting_Today_C ooke_Sharkey_Constructive_Leader_Impact.pdf

mistakes and place limits and rules on behaviors. Instead, leaders should inspire and coach team members and other leaders to find and understand the balance between tasks and individual needs.[46] They must help individuals through personal issues that may be encouraging them to disengage. Leaders must see and understand their impact on the culture. From there, they can correct defensive or aggressive behaviors where they see them.

---

[46] Robert A. Cooke and Linda Sharkey, "Developing Constructive Leader Impact," *Consulting Today,* 2006 (accessed Nov. 13, 2016). Available at ww.humansynergistics.com/Files/ResearchAndPublications/Consulting_Today_Cooke_Sharkey_Constructive_Leader_Impact.pdf.

CHAPTER 6
THE SEVEN ELEMENTS OF STRATEGY EXECUTION: THE TEAM

The team and the kind of people who comprise it are an essential element to executing strategy. Your organization is your people. Your people make its culture. It's your people, not the CEO and the executive team, who execute the strategy. Developing your organization into a team – whose collective and individual approach is goal attainment – takes superior management at all levels. It takes collaboration between units and desks, decentralized power and, critically, the right people.

i) The Right People

What do we mean by the *right people*? This is hiring and developing team members who support the strategy, believe in it and know where they fit in. The right people is the foundation for the execution of your organization's strategic plan. You can't build a high-performance team without people who fit your desired culture. Excellent communication is vital to helping team members see where they fit in and how the strategy is a win for them and the organization. Leaders must also recognize that having the right team members' means that some people in the organization may not be on board with the strategy. For whatever reason, they will not support it or believe in it. This issue must be identified and addressed early. You need everyone rowing together in the same direction.

The adage of hiring slow and firing fast remains relevant because it works. It is hiring for experience and qualifications, as you have always done, while placing a premium on fit. *Hiring slow* is something of a misnomer, because it does not mean intentionally dragging out your hiring process. It is being sure about a candidate's fit and being extremely selective in your hiring. In your decision-making, emphasize how this person fits into your strategy and the culture. What does the candidate bring to the strategy and the culture, and if so, where does it fit in? Will they "get" the culture, believe in the strategy and values? Can you see them being excited about the strategy, bringing a positive attitude, motivating others and thriving in a "we not me" environment? Or do you see this person thriving at the expense of others? You do not want an individual who excels by bringing down those around him or her. Hiring slow means including enough checks in your human resources processes to ensure you get someone who is the right fit. Aim for five, if not more, separate interviews with managers at various levels. Check references thoroughly and earlier in the process than at the negotiation stage. Through these conversations and gut checks at multiple levels, interviewers should be able to determine what the person would be like as a team member.

Senior managers should be directly involved in hiring. They can help see beyond the person's credentials and experience for an idea of their cultural fit. Larry Bossidy, co-author of *Execution: The Discipline of Getting Things Done*, looks for signs such as how excited the candidate is about doing things rather than talking strategy and philosophizing. Consider how much energy the candidate has brought to their accomplishments and how well they did them. Consider their execution as an individual and as a team player. What they emphasize in the interview may provide some indication of how they perform tasks in team environments. Do they provide examples of how much they have successfully motivated others? Bossidy also rightly suggests taking references seriously. Don't treat them as part of the rubber-stamping process after you've already decided on a candidate. Have the hiring manager, not human resources, call the references, and probe them for execution-related information that will inform your decision. Your best hire is not necessarily reflected in the best interview. You may very well learn more from the candidate's references and track record than you do from the face-to-face meeting.[47]

Just as hiring slow is an important discipline, so is firing fast. This is difficult for many organizations whose managers often prefer to shuffle non-team players into other roles or departments. However, organizations must see that if there's an error in hiring – and a team member isn't on board with the strategy or collaborating with colleagues – that person is effectively getting in the way of execution. As David Hopkinson outlines, if there is a lack of trust, collaboration or even passion and enthusiasm, they are an obstacle to your dedicated individuals and teams.[48] Everyone must be in agreement about the collective goal; if one team member disagrees, they can serve as a stressful, emotional drag on others' motivation and energy.

Greg McKeown, leadership consultant, explains it this way: "If 'hire slow, fire fast' sounds harsh or mercurial, consider how harsh it is to allow a whole team to be held hostage by someone who should not have been hired in the first place." Firing fast does not translate into a harsh dismissal. It should be done quickly for the good of the organization and the group – but humanely. Managers must have the courage to hold these difficult conversations and explain why the person is not the right fit for the role or the team. After bringing them around to your point of view, an agreement can be reached, perhaps with some career advice and coaching offered.[49]

Executives and managers must sustain excellent communications with all team members, especially those on the front line. These are the people executing the strategy. It's critical they understand it and are behind it. With constant, open communication, managers will find out relatively quickly if there are sticky team members who understand the strategy and how it

[44] Larry Bossidy, Ram Charan and Charles Burck, *Execution: The Discipline of Getting Things Done* (New York: Crown Business, 2002), 129–30.

[48] David Hopkinson, chief commercial officer, Maple Leaf Sports & Entertainment, interview with the authors (December 2014).

[49] Greg McKeown, "Hire Slow, Fire Fast," *Harvard Business Review,* March 3, 2014 (accessed May 20, 2017). Available at https://hbr.org/2014/03/hire-slow-fire-fast.

would benefit them but are still unable or unwilling to get on board with the strategy. These people must be identified quickly, and the difficult discussions had, because they are holding you back. If they're not part of your strategy execution, they're getting in the way of it.[50]

An organization changing strategic direction will almost necessarily experience changes to its talent, even the executive team. When changing strategies, be prepared to lose or let go of people you've worked with for years. While some people may outright disagree with the new strategy, others may not have the right skills or cultural fit. Say a national firm's new strategy involves adopting advanced client-facing technology and a new platform for direct, online engagement for sales and service. But the existing chief information officer, who has been with the organization for 15 years, doesn't have the know-how to implement the new technology. The rest of the executive team isn't sure he can learn it. An exit package may be more appropriate, to make way for a new CIO who fully understands the technology, the strategy and the culture objective.

High-performance cultures must be continually shaped, supported and reshaped. The investment in your people starts early and continues after their training and well into their careers. Strategy execution is not simply a case of management investing in the success of employees. That's part of it, but what you're really building is a culture where each employee is investing in each other's success. Collectively, they are all aiming for individual and group goal attainment and helping each other achieve it. Says Stephen Gunn, co-chief executive and co-founder of Sleep Country Canada: "If you hire people with good attitudes and you treat them right, it's powerful."[51]

---

[50] David Hopkinson, chief commercial officer, Maple Leaf Sports & Entertainment, interview with the authors (December 2014).

[51] Stephen Gunn, Sleep Country Canada, interview with the authors (August 2016).

ii) No Silos (Collaboration)

More than a quarter century ago, Jack Welch, then the Chairman and CEO of General Electric, had a vision for a need to break down silos. Technology and global markets were evolving so quickly that the pace of business decisions and operations couldn't keep up. He foresaw the pace of change only quickening, so that businesses would need greater collaboration and faster decision-making processes. Thus he came up with the GE Work-Out, a structure and process facilitating what he called the "boundaryless organization." Traditional organizational separations based on rank, department or geographic location went out the window and people got together in forums to problem-solve. Unfortunately, far too many organizations still operate with their people working in silos. They are making decisions within hierarchical structures and compartmentalized processes. Silos encourage a lack of information sharing, the protection of one's turf and, broadly, the erection of barriers that slow down or even halt your execution. Silos can be created and reinforced through processes but, ultimately, they are a mentality formed and sustained by management.

The GE Work-Out process was on to something. Welch envisioned an agile, collaborative corporate culture that gets things done. In a high-performance culture, people don't hide behind silos and processes – they jump in to problem-solve. What GE developed has been described as a process that tapped in to and reinforced "speedy problem solving, broad-based employee involvement and empowerment, open and direct dialogue between managers and subordinates, accountability, and continuous improvement."[52] When strategy execution is the collective priority, unhelpful processes are just another prob-

---

[52] William S. Schaninger, Jr., Stanley G. Harris and Robert E. Niebuhr, "Adapting General Electric's Workout for Use in Other Organizations: A Template," *Management Development Forum,* vol. 2, No. 1, 1999 (accessed April 1, 2017). Available at www8.esc.edu/ESConline/Across_ESC/forumjournal.nsf/0/c8c020477ee750cb8525 68fd0056cd61?OpenDocument.

lem-solving exercise for team members. In a collaborative, constructive culture, your people address the issue and move on toward the greater objective. They are loyal to the work environment and to each other's success and aim to improve that every day.[53]

In this workplace culture, there is no power base. The idea often feels counterintuitive to some traditional companies and organizations with long histories of executive power centers. Companies must not appoint executives and leaders who would reinforce or protect power bases. Executive offices like that of the CEO continue to exist, of course, but the idea here is that power is not *practiced*. While hierarchical offices may exist, the organization operates as a flat one. Inevitably, there will be people who feel their individual power base is threatened by new processes and collaborative or flat structures. Some people may try to undermine efforts for change as they protect the old silos or fiefdoms. These power bases can't exist. Where they are not aligned with your strategy and your culture, they are getting in the way of it.[54] Employees and executives alike must understand the culture, the strategy and their role in it. They must hold each other accountable if any power centers start to creep in, from the chief executive's office to the desks of frontline staff.

An organizational culture that's motivated and inspired keeps in check pressures that arise for silos or aggressive behaviors – which are often geared toward encouraging internal competition or protecting one's power base. They can manifest as behaviors such as taking charge and demanding loyalty, outperforming one's peers at the expense of the team, striving to attain narrowly defined and unrealistic objectives, or even nuanced behaviors like focusing on flaws rather than on successes and strengths. Recognize these as internally competitive behaviors that encourage silos and power bases. They are not healthy

---

[53] Chris Nickerson, senior vice president, sales distribution and marketing, NEI Investments, interview with the authors (October 2016).
[54] Baldev Seekri, *Organizational Turnarounds with a Human Touch*: Trafford Publishing, 2011), 155–60.

or achievement oriented. While organizations with these internally competitive behaviors can execute with some moderation, in excess they become pervasive, dominate the culture and run counter to performance. It's important to recognize them before they hold you back.

Reinforcing a no-silos, no–power base culture comes back to excellent communications, including listening. Leaders must repeatedly explain the strategy and its collective and individual benefits. Patrick Lencioni, author of *Silos, Politics and Turf Wars*, argues that your organization's cultural differentiation in the marketplace is more important than ever as companies are leaner, more competitive and looking for ways to eliminate frustration and waste.[55] So much of this cultural differentiation, he explains, is in communication: "The key to eliminating silos is simply to provide a compelling context for colleagues to understand that they should be rowing in the same direction. While leaders have been focusing on punishing negative behaviors that lead to internal conflict, they have often failed to give people a clear understanding of what they have in common, and why serving the common good is better for them than looking out for number one."[56]

The most successful organizational cultures are characterized by collaboration instead of silos. They accentuate achievement and strategy execution through individual development and teamwork. Employees are encouraged to be creative and to welcome responsibility. The culture instills a sense of ownership in their work and this results in a high degree of commitment and collaboration – not centers of power.

---

[55] Patrick M. Lencioni, *Silos, Politics and Turf War: A Leadership Fable about Destroying the Barriers that Turn Colleagues into Competitors* (San Francisco: Jossey-Bass, 2006).
[56] Patrick M. Lencioni, "Author Q & A Pat Lencioni - Silos, Politics and Turf Wars," The Table Group, 2014 (accessed April 16, 2017). Available at www.tablegroup.com/imo/media/doc/Author_QandA_Pat_Lencioni_Silos_Politics %20and%20Turf%20Wars.pdf.

iii) Self-Management Structure

If power bases have been holding back your organization, it's time to rethink structure. The organizational structure should be conducive to a constructive culture: collaboration, teamwork and shared goals. Today, pyramid-shaped organizational charts, with the boss at the top, are seen by many as wartime relics. They do not reflect the collaborative, practical working relationships between managers and staff. These old-fashioned pyramid charts are inherently dated. The top-down shape reflects a command-and-control approach, whereas in reality your organizational chart should probably look more like a flourishing garden. There may be different sections containing various types of vegetation, but everything is growing harmoniously to produce one greater effect. *Financial Times* columnist Andrew Hill conducted an informal survey on organizational charts and reports, and found: "Half of a small group of personnel directors I asked think such diagrams are an uncomfortable straitjacket, a loathed compliance obligation, a hindrance to more natural interaction between colleagues, or all three."[57]

There is new thinking about how to structure your organization for the best execution and results. More organizations are experimenting with Holacracy, a self-management, or self-organization approach. It replaces hierarchical structures with a peer-to-peer paradigm that redistributes power and aims to increase organizational agility, transparency, accountability and – of course – effectiveness.[58] Shoe company Zappos is adopting the system, with its CEO, Tony Hsieh, trying to understand how to make the organization behave more like a city than a big, unwieldy corporation. Hsieh says:

---

[57] Andrew Hill, "It Is Time to Kill the Org Chart," *Financial Times*, Dec. 12, 2016 (accessed April 30, 2017). Available at www.ft.com/content/2a477ad6-bc98-11e6-8b45-b8b81dd5d080

[58] See www.holacracy.org.

Research shows that every time the size of a city doubles, innovation or productivity per resident increases by 15 percent. But when companies get bigger, innovation or productivity per employee generally goes down. So we're trying to figure out how to structure Zappos more like a city, and less like a bureaucratic corporation. In a city, people and businesses are self-organizing. We're trying to do the same thing by switching from a normal hierarchical structure to a system called Holacracy, which enables employees to act more like entrepreneurs and self-direct their work instead of reporting to a manager who tells them what to do.[59]

The Holacracy approach is characterized by looser job descriptions so that employees are not defined by their titles and positions. Employees contribute in many ways and can fill more than one role. Decisions are made locally, rather than by managers who wield ultimate power. Teams self-organize instead of receiving instructions from higher up, and the same rules and transparency practices apply to everyone, including the chief executive.

Where an execution culture is driving your results, you do not need an old-fashioned hierarchical model. Instead, see your structure as flat. In truth, even the word *manager* is considered outdated. Within your organization, it is best replaced with *leader*, *coach* or some other word indicative of a team rather than hierarchy. But when you choose to do away with *managers* for *leaders* and *coaches*, ensure your organization's processes and culture also represent this shift. Employees will very quickly see hypocrisy where there's misalignment.[60]

---

[59] Zappos, "Holacracy and Self-Organization," Zappos Insights (accessed Dec. 18, 2016). Available at www.zapposinsights.com/about/holacracy.

[60] Curt W. Coffman and Kathie Sorenson, *Culture Eats Strategy for Lunch: The Secret of Extraordinary Results, Igniting the Passion Within* (Denver, Colo.: Liang Addison Press, 2013), 66.

iv) Multigenerations

As baby boomers retire, team members from very different age groups are beginning to work side by side. The retirement of an estimated ten thousand baby boomers per day in the United States, through at least the year 2030,[61] is poised to put tremendous strain on organizations unprepared for an accelerated need to fill leadership positions. In many cases, these management roles will be filled by candidates from much younger age groups, employees who may have starkly different priorities, areas of expertise and ways of looking at the world. If we were to believe the news headlines, millennials (born 1980 to 1995) are talented yet entitled, impossible to manage, difficult to please and sorcerers with technology. While some of these stereotypes may be true – that they are more educated, technologically competent and socially aware than previous generations – millennials are the next generation to lead companies. They make up a larger group than the generation ahead of them, Gen X. They also tend to be very well educated and entered the workforce at a suitable time to move into the leadership positions of retiring boomers.

Members of different generations may have very different working styles and preferences for achieving success. Millennials, having come of age with the Internet at their fingertips, tend to be "digital natives" who possess superior knowledge of communications, for instance. They are accustomed to the free flow of information. Many received constant parental supervision as they grew up, an experience reinforced by the instant gratification available on social media networks. Some members of the generation may "crave constant feedback and praise," [62] say researchers at the University of North Carolina's

---

[61] Glenn Kessler, "Do 10,000 Baby Boomers Retire Every Day?" *The Washington Post,* July 24, 2014 (accessed April 11, 2017). Available at www.washingtonpost.com/news/fact-checker/wp/2014/07/24/do-10000-baby-boomers-retire-every-day/?utm_term=.3fc70e7fe375.

[62] Dan Bursch and Kip Kelly, "Managing the Multigenerational Workplace," UNC Kenan-Flagler Business School, 2014 (accessed Jan. 28, 2017). Available at

Kenan-Flagler Business School. Baby boomers, on the other hand, developed their work experience in hierarchical environments with very constrained, rigid or compartmentalized information flows. This difference in working styles could be behind workplace conflict between millennials and baby boomers.

Leaders should ignore the stereotyped headlines about millennials and focus on the fact that this generation shares common goals with their elders. While they may have different priorities, their motivations are similar.[63] They want to learn, create value, receive recognition for their work and feel like they are contributing to something bigger than themselves. Priorities and the paths to goal achievement are different for every individual, no matter their generation. For leaders, the multigenerational question can be addressed relatively simply: Don't treat everyone alike.

Leaders must help team members establish goals that are aligned with personal success, while recognizing that rewards, compensation and coaching will be different for each employee. They must be tailored to that individual. Two employees from different generations may be working side by side and yet have completely different priorities. One may be happy to work overtime to put some additional savings away for retirement. The other may be thinking about implementing new technologies to cut back on unnecessary workplace processes while prioritizing work-life balance and spending more time with their young children. To find common drivers for team members of different generations, employees may be grouped, from a human resources perspective, into clusters of people with common needs and motivations. Personalizing rewards and employee goals can meet a broad spectrum of priorities. The differences within multigenerational teams are overstated. Em-

---

www.kenan-flagler.unc.edu/~/media/Files/documents/executive-development/managing-the-multigenerational-workplace-white-paper.pdf.
[63] Glenn Rifkin, "Engaging the Multigenerational Workforce," *Briefings Magazine,* Korn Ferry Institute, Feb. 24, 2016 (accessed Jan. 28, 2017) Available at www.kornferry.com/institute/engaging-the-multigenerational-workforce.

phasis should be on a common strategic goal that can unite team members across all stylistic differences.

CHAPTER 7
THE SEVEN ELEMENTS OF STRATEGY EXECUTION: ACCOUNTABILITY

The accountability piece of your execution culture reinforces trust, encourages open communication and keeps performance on track. You can't execute strategy effectively without openly discussing mistakes, shortfalls, wins and performance indicators. Everyone in the organization must feel they have the support of those around them. They must feel it is a team effort, that they can speak openly to one another about deficiencies, problem-solve together, own up to an error, learn from it and move on. Attempts at coordination or integration across divisions can suffer significantly if responsibilities are unclear or information isn't shared. We break down this section into four parts: how leaders set the example; how to build and grow trust; what to do with traditional performance reviews; and using a team scoreboard for tracking and improving results.

i) Accountability by Leaders

Accountability is very closely related to communication and leadership. Like the other aspects of your culture, people learn what's expected of them by the behaviors and attitudes of team leaders and executives. Great leaders have demonstrated that successful leadership is not tied to just what is said. It's what they do. Mahatma Gandhi, Martin Luther King Jr., Betty Friedan and Malala Yousafzai did not have an impact by thinking and speaking. They led by example.

Leaders must walk the talk if they are to build trust and show team members exemplary accountability. Vice presidents and senior leaders should call out the president and CEO if targets are missed, decisions diverge from the strategy or behaviors and processes are not aligned with the ideal culture. Where leaders unknowingly allow for poor sharing of information, inadequate knowledge transfer or unclear responsibilities, they unknowingly foster a culture obstructing your execution. Instead, their information-sharing processes, including their own responsibilities and accountabilities, must be transparent and open. They must be honest and crystal clear in their communications. Leaders should know that every action, process, reward and decision communicates something to the organization. Minute-by-minute, they must live and act out the behaviors they want to see in others. They must demonstrate accountability.

Leadership should be defined as the collective traits and actions of a leader. It is who they are and what they do. For better or worse, your organization's leaders pass on their behaviors to employees. Say a leader requests a meeting for a project update from his team but then misses the meeting without notice or explanation. What does this say to the group? That their time is not important. Another leader establishes a three-month target for a 30% sales gain of a new product, and with sales falling short, tells three divisions the deadline is inflexible but makes an exception for a fourth division, without explanation. What does this say? It fosters a culture of poor communication, distrust between team members and a belief that deadlines are arbitrary and unimportant. In each of these examples, leaders are not only cultivating a lack of trust but are also conveying that their requests to meet work demands aren't to be taken seriously.

Leaders must show employees how to take ownership. This is the feeling that the task you're completing is for you, your team and a bigger goal that everyone is striving to reach together. Feeling ownership over your work is quite contrary to an employee feeling they are "just a number" helping a large corporation expand its net income. Ownership goes back to nurturing and growing the leaders within for each of your team members. When employees feel ownership, they feel a desire to contribute to the strategy and further the goals of everyone involved. They take pride in their tasks. Ownership is both empowering for employees and a multiplier of the organization's accountability.

Leaders must continuously evolve, learn and teach, while demonstrating that the same level of accountability is expected of everyone. They ensure that teams are not held hostage by aggressive top performers – those who overshadow their team members as collective performance suffers. Would a basketball coach allow a star player to thrive at the expense of the team? Leaders must not make exceptions for those whose performance excels as they exhibit aggressive or disruptive behaviors not aligned with the culture. It's up to leaders to coach these top performers on how things should be done for the success of the team and the organization. Similarly, managers at all levels must understand that not all employees are top performers. The same level of accountability must be expected of everyone, top to bottom. Team members who are mediocre performers yet have the right cultural fit will do more to further execution than a few top people who outperform to the detriment of the culture. Find the right role suited to an employee's skills, and they will shine in a culture of trust and accountability.[64]

ii) Trust

For leaders, building a culture with strong accountability means building trust. This is done in many ways, but overall it is through open, honest communications and the transparent flow of information. When a leader makes a mistake or fails to complete a responsibility, they own up to it in a way that's transparent to their team and, if necessary, the entire organization. Employees do the same for their peers. If performance

---

[64] Greg Bustin, *Accountability: The Key to Driving a High-Performance Culture* (New York: McGraw-Hill Education, 2014), 532.

falls short of a target or a deadline is missed, the shortcoming is transparent to everyone and discussed in an open way. Interim results aren't executives' closely held secrets. Accountability is about everyone knowing where they are in their goals and understanding clearly what needs to be done to advance the strategy. Trust is believing in your colleagues and team leaders and knowing that you're supporting one another to advance the strategy.

Trust is very closely related to taking ownership. When everyone takes ownership of their roles and tasks, they trust one another to problem-solve and get the task done. When your culture fosters trust, trust is reciprocated between leaders and team members. Alphabet Inc. and other innovative organizations, like materials science company W.L. Gore and Associates, grant employees a certain portion of their time to work on their own ideas and pitches. This trust-building mechanism, this time for innovation, is provided without supervision and yields results in different ways. The staff are trusted to use the time to work toward pitching an idea, product or something of value for the organization. It was with this process – and a large amount of trust between employees and leaders – that W.L. Gore developed a versatile polymer we now commonly known as Gore-Tex.[65] A lack of trust, on the contrary, in colleagues or the company as a whole, often leads to turf protection, reduced initiative, shortcuts and, overall, slower decision-making. Trust is essential to developing highly engaged employees who are loyal to the strategy and the collective goal.[66]

Organizations with trust as a cultural trait employ people who are unafraid of failure. Fear of failure must not hold back your team members. They should feel empowered to take chances, use their judgment and problem-solve on their own where necessary. They are not afraid to be the first penguin in the water,

---

[65] James Heskett, *The Culture Cycle: How to Shape the Unseen Force That Transforms Performance* (Upper Saddle River, N.J.: FT Press, 2012), 181.
[66] James Heskett, *The Culture Cycle,* 136–7.

as the expression goes.[67] Encourage employees and leaders to not treat mistakes as mistakes. Instead, see them as corrections, where the team gets together to fix an issue and help out a team member who experienced a problem. Moreover, don't blame anyone. Mistakes are not the fault of an individual. They are the team's responsibility to correct and prevent from repeating in the future – not the individual's. Everyone learns from it and moves on. At the core of this process is trust: the ability of leaders and team members to collaborate, listen and enable multidirectional dialogue. In the backdrop, they have a clear line of sight on the strategy and, as a group, do not veer from the goal.

Groups with strong trust have strong bonds. They have the collective power to respond to outside threats created by competitors or unexpected events. Your people feel safe inside this group – not intimidated by any internal people or forces. This protection is what Simon Sinek author, motivational speaker and management theorist calls the Circle of Safety. Leaders should create and foster this circle around the organization to reduce any threats or oppositional forces people may feel within it. The culture will take its cues from the leader, reinforcing the circle. It effectively serves as a barrier, freeing up employees' time and energy to jump on opportunities as they arise and better protect the organization from outside threats that can drag down performance.[68]

iii) The Performance Review

Executives and managers should be continuously communicating their expectations for accountability. They must confront issues with performance quickly and head-on. It's a fundamental shift from the way organizations have typically reviewed team member performance. The traditional annual performance

---

[67] Chris Nickerson, senior vice president, sales distribution and marketing, NEI Investments, interview with the authors (October 2016).
[68] Simon Sinek, *Leaders Eat Last: Why Some Teams Pull Together and Others Don't* (New York: Portfolio / Penguin, 2014), 22.

review, where an employee's performance is critiqued and even scored, is no longer appropriate. In these annual reviews, managers often saved up negative comments about an employee's work, surprising the team member with an analysis of the totality of their shortcomings. The team member, rightly shocked, may walk away, thinking, "What a dishonest boss. Why didn't he tell me sooner? I'm looking for another job."[69] The manager, by failing to discuss performance with team members at regular, shorter intervals, has been communicating that they are either unaware of any issues or, worse, that they lack the courage to talk about them.

Your organization's team members know perfectly well who's performing and who isn't. Ignoring underperformance until the end of the year not only disregards your top performers, it's even insulting to them.[70] It communicates to everyone involved that the strategy doesn't *really* matter, that the company is satisfied with lackluster execution. Annual performance reviews should be an opportunity to celebrate wins with an employee and to discuss goals and their personal development. Perhaps it is also an opportunity to review any shortcomings that leaders have discussed with team members throughout the year. But the team member should come away from an annual performance meeting with deeper commitment and higher motivation.[71]

Individual performance should be evaluated continuously. If leaders are doing their jobs, employees clearly understand the strategy, the collective goal and how to get there. Through their performance reviews and more frequent checkups with their team leader, employees can identify their own personal goals as they align with the strategy. Maybe those goals include earning a certificate for a new skill, mastering an advanced piece of software or learning a new language. Whatever their goals, they know the strategy, their role in it and what's expected of them. When each team member understands the strategy at this

---

[69] Paul L. Marciano, *Carrots and Sticks Don't Work,* 121–2.
[70] Greg Bustin, *Accountability,* 530.
[71] Paul L. Marciano, *Carrots and Sticks Don't Work,* 122.

level, and receives continual feedback about their performance, accountability increases immensely as they hold themselves and others to goals and results.

Western Graphics, a small commercial printing company in Saint Paul, Minnesota, found it had cultivated a team of more engaged employees after it eliminated its biannual performance reviews. It replaced the reviews with "coaching conversations" every two weeks, supported by quarterly reviews. Almost right away, the company's results and performance increased. Western Graphics found that, while employees want to improve their contributions and be more productive, managers don't want to have to think about employee performance all year long. It's far easier for them to deal with performance issues as they're unfolding – or soon after – in a brief coaching meeting. This approach results in vast improvements for the team member, helping them understand their performance along the way. Moreover, the communication channels are opened more regularly, giving employees and leaders opportunities to focus on future goals rather than reviewing the past year.[72]

A culture of accountability reinforces positive behaviors and checks on performance regularly. Think of it as continuous coaching rather than frequent performance reviews. Both positive and negative feedback can be offered in one-on-one coaching moments, where the leader pulls the staff member aside to discuss a performance issue. If coaching opportunities don't arise naturally, leaders can schedule them about every two weeks. Short bits of positive, team-supporting feedback can be offered throughout the day. Ongoing communication is critical to team members' understanding of what they're doing well (or not well). The communication may be as simple as bringing a small distraction to their attention – even if it's an embarrassing personal issue. Paul Marciano, human relations consultant and author of *Carrots and Sticks Don't Work*, says he's been asked to inform executives about their halitosis, body odor or how their behavior was invasive to other team mem-

---

[72] Greg Bustin, *Accountability*, 650–1.

bers' workspaces. No successful sports team would wait until the postseason, or even the final minute of the game, to offer feedback. That is not winning tactics by any means.[73]

Team leaders, managers and executives will always have different styles and approaches to performance feedback. Overall, leaders should offer largely positive feedback that reinforces constructive behaviors aligned with the strategy. Marciano suggests an average split of 75% to 85% reinforcing positive feedback and 15% to 25% critical yet constructive feedback. He recommends that leaders avoid mixing positive and negative feedback. Deliver compliments about their work separately from corrective comments and, for an employee's personal performance, always offer negative, constructive feedback in private.[74] Consider it "constructive, focused feedback." It is not the same as criticism. Even when it points out a weakness, focused feedback should be positive. A feedback conversation might be as simple as reminding a team member about an upcoming deadline that has fallen off in priority. Use the opportunity to suggest not only improvements and solutions to shortcomings in performance, but also to any behaviors that aren't aligned with the culture.[75] The feedback helps team members stay focused on the strategy and the kind of behaviors that are encouraged.

iv) Results Dashboard

While leaders should focus on and repeat the strategy's most important messages, metrics should measure the strategy's most important tasks, behaviors and outcomes. The old saying holds true: No one pays attention to what the boss says but everyone pays attention to what the boss measures. You will have

---

[73] Paul L. Marciano, *Carrots and Sticks Don't Work*, 121–3; see also Don Clifton, *First, Break All the Rules: What the World's Greatest Managers Do Differently* (New York: Gallup Press, 2016), 247–8.
[74] Paul L. Marciano, *Carrots and Sticks Don't Work*, 124.
[75] Roger Connors and Tom Smith, *Change the Culture, Change the Game: The Breakthrough Strategy for Energizing Your Organization and Creating Accountability for Results* (New York: Penguin Group, Portfolio, 2011), 138–9.

a direct impact on the results you choose to measure. So, in other words, say what's important and measure it.

Many organizations have well-developed financial reporting capabilities. But, in most cases, the information reported does not adequately inform management or, worse, it encourages unwanted, misaligned behaviors. Performance measurement tools such as Balanced Scorecard – developed by Dr. David Norton and Dr. Robert Kaplan of Harvard University provides a comprehensive view of a company's performance and have their place in corporate management. But organizations should be aware these are not precision tools for driving engagement and a high-performance culture. In our research, we found leaders who were using the tool yet who reported problems trying to get everyone on the same page. Employee surveys are also good for measuring "how we do things around here" and organizational competency (what the organization's people know how to do), but they are not necessarily the right tool to drive engagement and execution.

While constant feedback helps to drive individual performance, metrics drive group performance. Use a team scoreboard to help set and sustain group expectations. Clear expectations about what team members should be doing in an average day keep them focused and help with the prioritization of tasks.[76] Have employees come to you because they are confused about which tasks to prioritize? This is a symptom of lack of focus and unclear expectations. Keeping a team scoreboard (a results dashboard) will put the strategy, and each team member's role within it, in their crosshairs. Team members need to understand very clearly the strategic goal ahead of them, how the team is going to execute it and what's expected of them on a daily basis. Tracking and providing public dashboard results weekly or even daily crystalizes this understanding for them. Performance transparency is critical to building trust, keeping teams focused and improving performance.

---

[76] Paul L. Marciano, *Carrots and Sticks Don't Work*, 149.

Steel producer Nucor Corp., for instance, sends team's dashboard reports each week with forward and backward looking data. Metrics show indications of safety, quality, productivity, sales and even profitability. Additionally, production metrics are posted at the end of each day, visible to everyone. A division with a lower rating on quality will be apparent company-wide, leading managers to call a meeting to discuss it, especially when the numbers show a trend. The performance metrics are not merely there for employees to ponder. Changes or trends in the data are points for analysis and discussion at meetings and can be used for rewards and compensation. Employees understand very clearly how performance bonuses are calculated, affecting their own contributions and behaviors. Teams are similarly rewarded for catching errors and, where an error is made, it's a team bonus that suffers, not an individual's.

When trying to decide what to measure for your dashboard, ask yourself: If your management team was a company unto itself, what key performance indicators would be vital, on a daily or weekly basis, to advancing the strategy?"[77]

Say a growing financial data provider has a strategy to become the fastest information-distribution service in the industry within three years. The strategy is clearly communicated to all teams. What then? It needs measurement. Essential to the firm's execution would be measuring the time lag between its data delivery and the delivery of its competitors. Who is reporting the data first, and by how many seconds or milliseconds? After figuring out how to measure this, the company communicates the gap weekly, perhaps even daily, to employees, using a consistent dashboard. Team members get a very real sense of the company's progress on the strategy. Any gaps observed in progress are an opportunity for meetings and discussion, and teams develop a much clearer picture of what they need to do to keep the strategy on track.

---

[77] Greg Bustin, *Accountability*, 431–47.

Your employees are motivated by progress, which can be represented in an information dashboard. They'll see the numbers – and work harder to improve them. Says Robert MacLellan, formerly of TD Bank Group:

> The great thing about measuring is not only the old thing of "what gets measured gets done," but also, if you measure things, you can celebrate victories. People need intermediate milestones to know they're winning, and if you're not measuring anything, it's hard to describe to people that you're winning. Part of having a positive culture is feeling like you're part of a winning organization.[78]

The dashboard should track whether short- and long-term goals, as part of the strategy, are progressing according to plan. Are sales increases on target? What about production and shipments? Allow team members to see how close they are to their targets, with updates at least every two weeks, depending on the goals. Employees need clear sight of what the goal looks like and why they're doing what they're doing. Perhaps meeting an intermediate goal by deadline means lowering quality defects by 3.5%, without any increased costs. That level of detail should be communicated to the group involved in production.[79] Data and numbers are critical to communicate goals and show success along the way.

Frequent meetings to discuss your results dashboard are important to celebrate successes and problem-solve any weaknesses. But use these meetings to also establish a rhythm of performance. Brief 20- to 30-minute meetings at the same time and place every week can create a feeling of rhythm among team members and a desire to sustain a high level of execution. Issues related to day to day functional operations should not be discussed at the meetings due to their distracting nature. Keep discussions focused on the strategy. Processes like these help create a rhythm, or "cadence of accountability,"

---

[78] Robert MacLellan, former TD executive, interview with the authors (March 2016).
[79] Paul L. Marciano, *Carrots and Sticks Don't Work*, 152.

in which a high level of execution is maintained. When the strategy is in focus, problems do not become excuses to abandon it. Instead, they are something to rally around, for the team to align and figure out. Establishing a rhythm of performance helps bring people together. It draws them toward one another for assistance, feedback, collaboration and ideas.[80]

---

[80] Chris McChesney, Sean Covey and Jim Huling, *The 4 Disciplines of Execution*, 80–1.

CHAPTER 8
THE SEVEN ELEMENTS OF STRATEGY
EXECUTION: SYNERGY

So, your team members understand the strategy. They work with strong behaviors of accountability. They're collaborative, innovative, energized and focused. Now what? Synergy is linking it all together. It's ensuring teams and units have the right infrastructure and structures to get the job done. If the culture is right, execution gains momentum quickly. Synergy is the grease that enables the key elements to work together because, when they do, the power is much greater than the sum of the parts.

i) Program Synthesis

The strategic plan is not in itself a goal – it is too big to be a goal. It's better described as a large project that needs to be broken down, cascaded into departments, groups, programs and their attendant goals. A project manager is necessary to ensure the strategic plan – in this case, the project – is unpacked and organized into manageable programs for each relevant department and section. Depending on the size of the project, these programs are typically divided again into smaller programs, while still supporting each department or section's broader goal within the strategy. The importance here for the project manager is not simply to create a project charter – with a business case, high-level timelines and budget controls – it is to ensure that all programs are aligned. Your business units, divisions and teams have probably defined success, at one time or another, as projects that finished on time and under budget. That approach, although it illustrates satisfactory execution, is not high-performance strategy execution.

Your project manager is not outside help whose job it is to simply ensure the deliverables are received on time and under budget. She must be part of the team and the culture, and a champion of the strategy. Preferably, the project manager is an internal leader or executive who understands the strategy and culture objective. She reports to the sponsor of the strategy (usually the CEO or a high-level executive) and is a leader in behaviors, culture and performance. Like the rest of the leadership team, the project manager helps communicate the why of the project and the strategy. She hears from department and section heads about any snags in operations, sales, HR or IT, hurdles that could slow down the strategy. She ensures each respective department has the resources and additional staff needed to make the strategy happen.

We recommend conducting a review of your organization's portfolio of programs. Do they all point to a single strategic plan and vision? Goals for each program must be divided, categorized, reevaluated and rewritten so that they are clearly defined as part of the strategy. Each team member and department understands the goals across the organization and the importance of each program and strategic initiative.

Say Company A, a large American firm of ten thousand employees, develops a strategic plan to expand its business into Europe, with a large office in Berlin. The CEO is responsible for the strategy, making her the sponsor. The plan is cleared by the legal and finance departments and the reason for the strategy is clear – the European market has shown the fastest-growing demand for the company's services. The CEO appoints a member of her executive team as the project manager. The project manager sees that the strategy is appropriately broken down into parcels of work, or programs, for each department and section. The project charter, with a schedule of work, quality controls and a budget, helps serve as a guide for each department, group and section.

The project manager needs to embrace what consultant Ken Robertson calls "progressive elaboration" – the notion that we learn and adapt as the project progresses, adjusting and solidifying the plans, costs and expectations.[81] Say Company A, after deploying the project charter for its expansion to Europe, finds that its IT department immediately complains it needs hardware, additional service expertise and, most important, nearly a doubling of staff. Next, the sales team starts to feel overwhelmed. Right away, the project manager needs to recognize that the strategy is creating a huge amount of additional work for IT, sales and, as a consequence of the expansion, HR. It's not the project manager's job to simply ensure these departments get enough resources and the budget to hire staff. They need help communicating why the expansion is happening, the benefits of it for all existing and incoming team members and what the end goal looks like. The project manager needs buy-in from key departments – in this case, IT, sales and HR. They are critical to the strategy and need to be behind it as champions.

The project manager's role is a crucial one in synthesizing the portfolio of programs and connecting them to the strategic plan and the culture. They can't just create a schedule of work, drive it to completion, and then dust off their hands. They would walk away leaving the CEO with very unhappy sales, IT and HR teams – and a degraded culture with serious performance consequences over time. Instead, the project manager helps synthesize bundles of work. Employees and leaders should be able to link each program, however big or small, directly to the strategy. Goals are aligned with the strategy and cascaded into each program to ensure timelines are reached. Measurement is introduced to motivate teams and ensure progress is on track. Throughout this process, the project manager is integral to two-way communication about the strategy – both down from the CEO and up from the front lines. Good project managers understand the value that their project is delivering. They are

---

[81] Ken Robertson, "Business Outcome Management," in David Barrett and Derek Vigar, Eds., *Keys to Our Success: Lessons Learned from 25 of Our Best Project Managers* (Oshawa, Ont.: Multi-Media Publications Inc., 2013), 167–77.

fully behind it and serve as another voice within the leadership who helps to energize and focus teams.

A big part of synergy is ensuring alignment, not just in your portfolio of programs but in the less obvious pieces of the strategy and the organization. A big part of creating synergy is ensuring that *everything* is aligned. That includes the organization's structure, processes and rewards – they should all point in the same direction. Structure, for instance, should not contradict processes. A flat hierarchical structure facilitates communication and focused feedback in both directions. Does the CEO hold a company-wide meeting once per year or quarter? At the meetings, does he simply give a speech? Or take employee questions for an hour? Do your processes also facilitate communication and feedback? Team members will laugh in amazement if an IT department can't get authorization from management to upgrade terribly outdated software that is necessary to the strategy. Do your rewards align with the culture, encouraging teamwork and constructive behaviors? Or do they promote individualism? Small details can speak volumes about how your organization does things. Think carefully about each aspect of your organization. Be sure it is aligned – and that you have the capacity to align it before starting out.

ii) Are We Achieving Our Goals?

Daily or even real-time performance feedback communicated through a dashboard or regular feedback channels keeps employees on top of their goals. Clear and continuous communication lets employees know what's expected of them. Crystal clear expectations are a big part of finding and sustaining synergy. And when you have synergy, all team members set expectations for one another. Leaders should continue to contribute to the culture in a constructive way by correcting behaviors when they're not aligned with the culture and values. They should leave no doubts about expectations and show that the small things matter. When assigning a task, for instance, put it in writing. No employee wants to guess at what they are supposed to be doing because they are too embarrassed to ask for a reminder about the details of their tasks.[82] Be sure employees have opportunities and a venue to ask questions and provide feedback. The channels should be open.

When starting on a new project, create not only intermediate goals but also hold progress meetings, or checkpoints, for evaluation of how things are going and any available data indicating progress. Front-load this process with more checkpoint meetings at the beginning of the strategy's implementation. These give you ample opportunity for corrective actions at the start, when there are more likely to be problems. When your teams are working fast, they can make significant headway on a program before finding out they're headed in the wrong direction.[83] These progress meetings are early markers; they are important because they ensure programs are on schedule and progressing according to plan. They are also an occasion to energize teams as they collectively move the ball forward. Very clear expectations have been communicated to them – so let them know precisely where they are in the journey.

iii) Living Well and Having Fun

No company wants to be the "unfun" place to work. On the contrary, you want a culture that makes execution enjoyable. Your people should come to work and have fun – literally. That doesn't mean coming to the office and spending the day playing table tennis or going for a four-hour, boozy lunch. Sometimes it might. Most of the time, employees feed off a positive, forward-leaning energy within the group. Human workplace expert Liz Ryan describes it as a lightness that team members can feel in the air. Nothing feels heavy. Even with very serious work ahead of them that is necessary to execute the strategy, the culture has a buoyancy and weightlessness to

---

[82] Paul L. Marciano, *Carrots and Sticks Don't Work,* 158.
[83] Paul L. Marciano, *Carrots and Sticks Don't Work,* 159.

it. People have fun. Within their organizational culture, they feel the good intent of everyone they're working with.[84]

A happy workplace is important to ensuring your people have fun. While your culture will make for a fun environment, allow team members to prioritize their own well-being and self-care when necessary. Allow employees time for mental health days and family needs and provide them with opportunities to build work relationships. Those who overextend their personal limits for career success can eventually underperform, perhaps withdrawing during stressful times when the team needs them most. Individuals with more balanced lives and energy, however, thrive and rise to the occasion when demands peak. Organizations need this resiliency on their teams. There will certainly be unexpected occasions when teams need to pull together to react to an event or meet a big deadline. Emma Seppälä, author of *The Happiness Track: How to Apply the Science of Happiness to Accelerate Your Success*, says allowing time for self-care and building positive relationships is career-boosting. Employees will appreciate the time and in the end demonstrate more resilience and success.[85]

There is a balance to be struck between the needs of your people and the need to get things done. If your culture is constructive and healthy, workplace flexibility should enhance your execution, not come at the expense of it. Leaders often encourage or approve of passive and defensive behaviors such as employees emphasizing people over tasks, withholding critical feedback, taking a "company is always right" mentality, choosing safety over risk or generally approaching decisions in an approval-seeking way. This leadership is harmful to your culture when it's excessive.

---

[84] Liz Ryan, "How to Have Fun at Work," *Forbes.com,* Aug. 18, 2014 (accessed Jan. 18, 2017). Available at www.forbes.com/sites/lizryan/2014/08/18/how-to-have-fun-at-work/#6ada2fce73c9

[85] Emma Seppälä, "Being Happier at Work," *Harvard Business Review,* Jan. 28, 2016 (accessed Jan. 18, 2017). Available at https://hbr.org/ideacast/2016/01/being-happier-at-work.

A survey of hundreds of managers found that leaders who have the most constructive impact within their organizations tend to manage in "prescriptive" ways. Rather than emphasizing mistakes, they guide and coach people toward goals and focus on what's being done right. They highlight what employees and the organization desire while vocalizing and facilitating constructive, productive behaviors. Employees free their leaders within, acting and making independent decisions more liberally.[86]

Your culture, ultimately, will determine whether people enjoy being at work. That said, there are always ways for extra fun that can be combined with team-building – and contribute to synergy. Charitable team challenges are a good way to gather team members in a setting outside the office, and for a good cause. Or consider hiring a photographer to take team photos (and some silly ones), then share them on your company social media pages. Fitness activities can combine team-building, fun and health. Consider a company sports team in an inclusive sport like softball. And don't forget social events. Monthly catered lunches with social time for mixing can be beneficial.[87] With any of these activities, it's important for team members to have fun while constructively reinforcing the culture. Don't force such events on people – especially if a defensive or aggressive culture exists, with mistrust. The activities can worsen the culture if there has not been an effort to openly and honestly improve trust and accountability. Without this effort, events aimed at "having fun" send a message that the company cares more about the appearance of a happy workplace than a happy one.[88]

---

[86] Robert A. Cooke and Linda Sharkey, "Developing Constructive Leader Impact."
[87] Jacqueline Whitmore, "The Surprising Benefits of Having Fun at Work," *Entrepreneur*, Jan. 31, 2017 (accessed March 4, 2017). Available at www.entrepreneur.com/article/288223.
[88] Liz Ryan, "How to Have Fun at Work."

iv) Scalability

To execute your strategic plan, you need to be ready for what your strategy will create. Strategy execution can't happen solely on willpower and leaders within. You also need to empower your teams with the right expertise, processes, systems, technology and structures. Your people may be believers in the strategic plan, ready to drive toward an ambitious growth goal, but if you don't give them the tools and resources to do it, they will fail. This is common with start-ups that grow too fast. They don't have the scalability necessary to meet surging demand for their products or services. Perhaps they can't find the right talent or, worse, don't know where to look for it. Having scalability is understanding what you are creating. You must have the means – not just the drive – to meet outside pressures and demands that will come from executing at a high level.

The first thing you need is a solid organizational infrastructure. Your infrastructure is how you set up your group. It covers everything from roles and authority structures to the guidelines and rules that help set expectations and behaviors. Your people are also a big part of your infrastructure. You need human resources processes in place to ensure the right people are in the right positions, that the right talent is hired and that, overall, people are in the roles they flourish in. Talent is critical. If you're a tech company offering software created from a specific programming skill, do you have enough expertise to significantly scale up what you're offering? You need to know that you can deliver what you're promising. Scalability is planning and knowing that your scale is flexible enough to win bigger deals or orders than you may have expected.

Elon Musk, chief executive of Tesla Motors and known for ambitious business plays, once made a bet on Twitter that he could deploy a power system in Australia – within 100 days – to fix problems with energy shortages and blackouts in South Australia. Expected or unexpected, Australian technology billionaire Mike Cannon-Brookes took him up on the Twitter offer: to use Tesla batteries to provide the storage for as much as 300 megawatt hours of energy. "Tesla will get the system installed and working 100 days from contract signature or it is free," Musk promised on Twitter. Good public relations aside, can the company actually deliver it? In all likelihood, Tesla can, but companies must be aware of their capacity to scale up significantly if they are going to make big bets aligned with their strategy.[89]

Your organization must have the necessary infrastructure and processes in place. Your people and teams must be ready to scale up, fast, if necessary, to support the strategy. Say a technology-components manufacturer receives a new client that suddenly expands the company's product sales by 40%. What if the teams on the factory floor are ready to go, but the company's cobalt supplier can't provide enough cobalt? Firms must plan for scalability. Can your wholesale purchasing processes scale up? Are your internal accountability mechanisms sufficient to handle excess demand? Is your regulatory compliance department set up for an expanded mandate? Ensure there's a plan in place in the event that processes and procedures need to run bigger and faster.

Your new strategy may require new technology. Scalability involves adopting the right solutions to support execution. Ensure any necessary technology is in place and teams have been trained to use it before marketing it to large customers. It's possible your strategy may require special talents. Be sure there are qualified people in the job market available for hire – and who fit with your culture. Say a software technology company has a strategic plan for its new product. Sales are going well. But then its biggest client calls for a major new order and asks that the platform be tweaked to perform something its designers did not anticipate. The platform needs some reprogramming. Does the company have the talent internally to make it happen? Otherwise, they may have sold something they can't deliver. Your production trajectory must be able to

---

[89] Perry Williams, "Musk Bets He Can Fix Aussie Power Woes in 100 Days or It's Free," Bloomberg News, March 10, 2017 (accessed March 19, 2017). Available at www.bloomberg.com/news/articles/2017-03-10/musk-bets-he-can-fix-aussie-power-woes-in-100-days-or-it-s-free.

meet your growth trajectory. If not, you can't scale your business, and execution will stall.

Outsourcing is an important aspect of scalability planning. Anticipate where you can outsource tasks and jobs if necessary. Organizations that do not have the ability to scale quickly internally should at least have a plan to scale using external sources. When outsourcing, make an effort to protect the culture. Organizations do not want external teams coming in and disrupting the culture they have carefully crafted. An acceptable solution is to try to limit outsourcing to automation and tasks that aren't necessarily performed in-house. Many companies and factories offer automated production, 3-D printing and even machine-learning robots for rent. Don't let external teams disrupt the culture – and remind yourself that your people are your greatest asset.

Be realistic in your timelines. A key part of scalability is taking a cautious approach to growth. Your strategic plan is probably a good idea – so good that you may scale too fast. Adopt a timeline that allows you to grow at an ambitious but not alarming rate. Surprise orders and deals are good when they're within your capabilities. Come up with a plan to scale up to meet your strategic plan at a certain rate and align your projects and goals according to the same pace. Be sure all teams – and the organization's portfolio of projects – are aligned on the same timeline. You do not want one department to fall behind the others as demand picks up. To be sure, when you develop the right culture, ensure there is alignment across the organization.

v) Quality

Capacity and scalability, as part of generating synergy, are linked to quality. While capacity and reasonable growth timelines should be on your checklist, so should quality. Leaders focused on building a constructive execution culture to support a new strategy can use the opportunity to shape not just a high-performance environment but also a culture of quality. This is a culture where employees don't just follow guidelines, they exceed them. They hear their colleagues talking about quality, see them focusing on quality and take actions to improve quality. It becomes another point of pride for employees, a competitive achievement to celebrate. An added benefit of quality is lower costs. For every error an organization makes, there are direct costs associated with fixing it, let alone any damage to your brand.[90]

Toyota Motor Manufacturing Inc.'s Kentucky plant, its largest in the United States, is an example of quality playing a consequential role in the culture. The company says its high employee engagement is a result of guiding principles and a corporate culture that supports individual creativity, values teamwork and, important, puts quality on a pedestal. The seven-thousand-member team has the capacity to produce fifty thousand vehicles per year, plus service parts, amounting to sales of more than $10 billion per year. Employees are encouraged to make decisions that ensure superior quality. Says Wilbert W. James, president of the plant: "At Toyota, we think about culture every day. One of the basic tenets of Toyota … [is what we call] the 'Toyota Way' – everybody working together to produce the highest quality car at the lowest cost. It takes people working together and trusting one another to make it happen…. We're constantly monitoring the morale of our workforce and communicating, actively getting them to engage and get their suggestions on the table. We empower team members on the line."[91]

---

[90] Ashwin Srinivasan and Bryan Kurey, "Creating a Culture of Quality," *Harvard Business Review,* Apr. 2014 (accessed Oct. 1, 2016). Available at https://hbr.org/2014/04/creating-a-culture-of-quality.
[91] Yvette Caslin, "Toyota Motor Manufacturing President Wil James Talks Culture and Employee Engagement," *Rollingout,* Apr. 8, 2013 (accessed Oct. 1, 2016). Available at http://rollingout.com/2013/04/08/toyota-motor-manufacturing-president-wil-james-talks-culture-and-employee-engagement.

CHAPTER 9
THE SEVEN ELEMENTS OF STRATEGY EXECUTION: THE PLAN

From the outset of this book, we've assumed you have a solid, sensible strategic plan for your organization. You've laid out the strategic road map, identified the value you're bringing to the marketplace and ensured your people and stakeholders are on board with the plan. You've aligned your strategic priorities with industry trends and the needs of customers. But your strategic plan is not enough. You also need a plan of execution. This is where your culture comes in, and the tactics, processes, infrastructure and people supporting the execution. Your strategic plan necessarily involves a plan of execution – with unwavering focus on the strategy.

i) Goals: Knowing Where We're Headed

You have a sound strategy. Perhaps it is expanding to another jurisdiction, launching a new product or using new technology to overtake a competitor's market share. Whatever your strategic plan, it must be clear to employees and, to help clarify it, you need goals aligned with it. After establishing your strategic objective and long-term goals, set in place strategic milestones that advance the strategy over the near and medium term, then finally to its conclusion. Set targets for your operating plans while making sure that your processes, structures, rewards and milestones are aligned with the strategy.[92]

---

[92] Bossidy, Charan and Charles Burck, *Execution*, 148–9.

Without goals, your team members don't really know what's expected of them. Clear, realistic and yet ambitious goals are vital to executing the strategy. Ensure that the supporting infrastructure and resources are in place to support those goals.[93] Save your organization the embarrassment of setting an ambitious sales target for the end of the quarter if there's a chance that, halfway through the period, your supply chain may be able to deliver only three-quarters of what you need. Additionally, set challenging goals. Be ambitious yet realistic. If you do decide to set targets that are slightly out of reach, communicate that decision to the organization and see what everyone can do.

It's vital to communicate goals with intermediate targets and the why behind them. The benefits of clear goals are that employees get satisfaction from and feel driven by coming in every day knowing what they're working toward and how far they've come on a daily or weekly basis. It's the difference between trying to get somewhere in a big city without a map versus arriving there swiftly with GPS navigation.[94] Your goals are like directions. Employees will know what to prioritize day-to-day and how to recognize problems and obstructions along the way.

Attach numbers to goals that can be measured through weekly or even daily metrics. To reach that goal of a 10% sales increase by the end of the quarter, perhaps there's a need to sustain an average of fifteen thousand sales per week. Metrics should make it very transparent to team members whether they are delivering this number weekly; if they're not, team leaders must be communicating with team members about what needs to change to make it happen. Goals should be written down, put on the record and communicated for everyone to see.

Employees should have a strong picture in their minds of what success looks like. What does it mean to meet this goal? Visualizations can help solidify it. Perhaps it's something as simple as a party hat that is visible with a big "2" on it, a reminder to

---

[93] Paul L. Marciano, *Carrots and Sticks Don't Work*, 145–6.
[94] Paul L. Marciano, *Carrots and Sticks Don't Work*, 145–9.

everyone about the company lunch on March 2 to celebrate a goal accomplishment. Leaders can show employees a picture of what it is they're working toward. If they're working on a report, distribute a sample design of what it should look like.[95] Come up with a tentative title for it, and a cover image. None of it needs to be definitive – the point is to help them visualize what it is they're working toward.

Develop a vision or mission statement aligned with the strategy and goals. The vision does not have to be too detailed. It's not meant to be attainable, but it should be descriptive enough that employees can see what ultimate success would look like. Martin Luther King Jr.'s "dream," for instance, was sufficiently descriptive that his followers could picture it. Someday, according to his vision, "little black boys and black girls will be able to join hands with little white boys and white girls as sisters and brothers."[96] The vision should provide team members with something to aspire to. It's aligned with the strategy and your values. It may never be reachable in your practical outlook, but everyone is willing to try, giving it their all.

Leaders should not devise goals in closed-door meetings with executives. Try discussing them at a town hall. Form committees. Involving your employees in the setting of goals and targets goes a long way to creating buy-in. If team members feel new goals are being hoisted upon them from upper management, they're likely to resent what's being asked of them. But when they feel they are part of the organization's new strategic direction and goals, they feel like they are pursuing their own objectives.[97]

This is an important distinction. Leaders do not want their employees to feel that short- and mid-term targets are the only goals. Targets help to focus employees and teams but they can also be dangerous if team members become singularly focused on them. An inflexible approach to goals and associated mone-

---

[95] Paul L. Marciano, *Carrots and Sticks Don't Work,* 153.
[96] Quoted in Simon Sinek, *Leaders Eat Last,* 43.
[97] Daniel H. Pink, *Drive,* 165.

tary rewards by employees can result in shortcuts that impair ethical, quality or safety standards.[98] The last thing leaders want is targets and goals that unintentionally incentivize behaviors running counter to the ideal culture. It's extremely important that your goals, vision and rewards are aligned with the culture. Your culture, and the accountability within it, should immediately single out any lapses in behavior. Indeed, it's your culture and the satisfaction of daily tasks and contributions that make the activity of work the true reward for employees.

ii) Vision and Values

Your values and vision are a key piece of your plan of execution. Have them in place before launching execution, because they work in tandem with the goals and strategic milestones along the way. Your values statement should reflect what your organization stands for and what it contributes, while your vision is a kind of ultimate goal, one that is not necessarily realistic or practical but something everyone can get behind and strive toward. Values and vision may need to be updated over time to keep in alignment with the strategy in a changing marketplace. If they aren't aligned, there will be consequences; in fact, it would better to have no values or vision. Employees pick up on any hypocrisy, posing a threat to the culture. Your culture is another reason to involve employees in the value- and vision-writing process: It increases ownership over their work and creates a clearer picture of why they're doing what they're doing.

Your values are an opportunity to present positive, constructive attributes of your ideal culture and strategy. They can be just a few words reminding employees of your organization's cultural objectives. Retailer Build-A-Bear Workshop, a plush toy company based in Missouri, rather cutely describes its core values as: "Reach, learn, di-bear-sity, colla-bear-ate, give and

---

[98] Daniel H. Pink, *Drive,* 49–50.

cele-bear-ate."[99] While amusingly working the bear theme into its values, the company is, in actual sense, bringing employees' attention to very tangible, constructive cultural objectives like collaboration, embracing diversity, learning and progression. A vision gives team members a nobler purpose, an aspirational goal that the strategy advances. Whole Foods Market, for instance, describes its vision as a "higher purpose statement," comprised of the following: "With great courage, integrity and love – we embrace our responsibility to co-create a world where each of us, our communities and our planet can flourish. All the while, celebrating the sheer love and joy of food."[100]

iii) Commitment Translated to Action

Employees may be committed to the strategy and the plan – but that commitment needs to flow through to action. A healthy company and culture, and the actions that comprise execution, begin with purpose. Do your employees have purpose? They should; if not, you should help them find one. Your vision, values and the ideal culture should be communicated so that team members find purpose in their tasks, no matter the task. Profits or monetary rewards are not a purpose. Ultimately, if this is their greater goal, it will leave them unsatisfied, unfulfilled and unmotivated. What they need is purpose related to learning, growing and improving. It is essentially a social objective, one that contributes to a happier, more creative team environment and in the end a healthier society. This is what drives people.[101] Understand that each and every team member must feel they have an intrinsic purpose or goal.

Focused feedback provided at regular intervals helps motivate people and keep them dedicated to the culture and the strategy. Team leaders should work on drawing out each person's leader within. Finding the commitment of a leader within is giving a

---

[99] Build-A-Bear Workshop, "Why You Should Become a Bear" (accessed May 24, 2017). Available at https://careers.buildabear.com/AboutUs.aspx.
[100] Whole Foods Market, "Our Core Values" (accessed May 24, 2017). Available at www.wholefoodsmarket.com/mission-values/core-values.
[101] Daniel H. Pink, *Drive,* 142–5.

person the independence to make decisions and problem-solve. They are free to take action and make decisions that advance the strategy. It's where the company's people have an eagerness to do a lot more than "letter of the law" compliance to perform their job descriptions and functions. When a leader within is engaged, the team member is engaged rationally *and* emotionally. They are motivated to activate what they've learned and they have a willingness to invest discretionary effort to make things happen.

A committed employee who can problem-solve on their own and act independently when necessary is engaged rather than motivated. Motivation is what drives an employee toward a short-term reward, like a cash bonus. An engaged team member, on the other hand, is driven not by carrots but by the positive culture and the greater goal. They are motivated by their own team contribution, creativity and accomplishments rather than something purely for themselves. A critical difference between an engaged employee versus a motivated one is their behavior in an economic downturn or a negative working environment. The engaged team member pushes through it, working with others to change their circumstances and works harder to reach their goals, while the motivated employee disengages in unfavorable circumstances.[102]

iv) Agility

As part of your execution plan, you must be ready to act quickly. Organizations today must have the ability to move fast, to adapt and change according to unexpected threats and shifting environments. This may mean adapting your strategic goals to embrace technological changes or take advantage of unexpected developments. Your people and your collaborative culture meet most of the need to adapt. With purpose in their work and the culture empowering their leaders within, they will make independent decisions on the frontline that make your organization much more flexible and agile.

---

[102] Paul L. Marciano, *Carrots and Sticks Don't Work,* 40–1.

Culture alone does not completely solve agility issues, however. The right processes and structures can facilitate quick decision-making. Establish your processes and organizational infrastructure so that they enable collaboration and team problem-solving. Committee structures should not reinforce silos. Passing decisions down vertically, from upper management to heads of divisions and then to division teams, encourages silo mentality. Team members must feel they are collaborating and being included in problem-solving. Horizontal committees should have the ability to assemble in a snap and make decisions quickly. Do not confuse agility, however, with a flexible or agile structure. Quite the contrary – your processes and structure, while enabling agility, should be strong and stable. Team members, when regularly reacting to outside change and threats, want to feel as though they are doing so from a very safe and stable home base.[103]

People want to feel comfortable and safe at work, where they are among friends. Although flat organizational structures can be used to support collaboration and feedback, friendly, constructive hierarchies, with coaches and leaders above, also remain important. Employees often want to feel that they have leaders who are looking out for them. Instead of having large silos or divisions, think of breaking the organization into communities of fewer than 150 people. Why 150? The number is seen as important because people can't establish meaningful relationships with a group beyond this size. Bill Gore, founder of W.L. Gore and Associates, discovered this in his production of materials and fabrics. He found his most effective plants were comprised of fewer than 150 employees and that those employees experienced exceptional camaraderie and teamwork. The bigger factories were less efficient because the culture was less constructive.[104] Capping each community at 150 creates stronger bonds, trust and support between members

---

[103] Interview, McKinsey principals Wouter Aghina and Aaron De Smet, "The Keys to Organizational Agility," McKinsey & Company, December 2015 (accessed March 9, 2017). Available at www.mckinsey.com/business-functions/organization/our-insights/the-keys-to-organizational-agility.

[104] Simon Sinek, *Leaders Eat Last*, 112–3.

of the group. Ideally, your people come to work and spend the day with friends, not just colleagues. Having this security of a friendly community significantly increases your capacity for agility and faster responses. The stronger the community, the stronger the teamwork and the better the team's ability to respond to threats or changing environments.

As you look at ways to improve your agility, consider a review of your entire ecosystem. You may be surprised what you find. The ecosystem includes all of your major systems and sections, including human resources, logistics, services, IT and finances. How would potential threats or emerging issues affect each section of the company? How are they managed, and what are their biggest weaknesses and opportunities? Teams and committees should meet in person to encourage feedback and brainstorming. Don't forget your customers. To remain agile, always be ready to learn, and there is much to learn from external sources. Listen to clients, customers and contractors who have an outside view. They are likely to offer a much different perspective about any emerging trends coming your way.[105]

v) Flexibility

While your strategy is paramount and your focus on it unwavering, a big part of your execution plan is flexibility. This does not refer to a rethink of your entire strategy when things aren't working out. However, it may mean the *how* of your strategic goal is adjusted along the way.

TD Bank found itself in this situation in the late 1990s when it was executing a strategic plan to expand its retail services through the acquisition of Canada Trust. Charles Baillie, the bank's chairman, oversaw the TD–Canada Trust merger at the time, which represented a large strategic shift in TD's business from wholesale to retail banking. Initially, TD planned to absorb Canada Trust's retail business while cutting a head office,

---

[105] Amanda Setili, *The Agility Advantage: How to Identify and Act on Opportunities in a Fast-Changing World* (San Francisco: John Wiley & Sons, 2014).

along with other efficiencies. But the amalgamation didn't quite go as planned. Canada Trust's retail services, and its frontline service culture, was so strong that TD recognized cost cutting would not be aligned with the expansion of the retail banking. Robert MacLellan, chief investment officer with TD at the time, explains: "After the transaction closed, what we found was that the Canada Trust people were really, really good retail bankers. It was all they did. They knew it well, they were passionate about it, and they were very promotional." Small things like calling their ATMs "cash machines" and offering longer branch hours than other banks were parts of the Canada Trust culture that gave it superior retail services.[106]

Canada Trust's culture of customer service was so strong that, when TD took a closer look at what it had acquired, it decided to align its strategy with the people. Cost cutting Canada Trust's excellent retail services would not have been aligned with the culture or the strategy. Instead of cutting tellers and other retail expenses, the company realigned its strategy with the Canada Trust culture: It would become the best at retail banking. Canada Trust had higher banking fees, but TD recognized that customers accepted them because the service was superior. TD instead repriced its fees to be in line with those of Canada Trust. Profits rose significantly after the merger, and this increase was not based on the initial plan to reduce expenses. Instead, profits grew on revenue synergies and a strategy that was aligned with the culture. "As a result of that merger, bank profits went way up, but they didn't go up for the reason we thought. They didn't go up because we thought we'd be able to take out expenses, they went up because we had revenue synergies. In mergers, revenue synergies are the absolute holy grail," MacLellan recalls.[107]

---

[106] Robert MacLellan, former TD executive, interview with the authors (March 2016)

[107] Robert MacLellan, former TD executive, interview with the authors (March 2016); see also Dan Ovsey, "Behind the Scenes of TD Canada Trust's Cultural Evolution," *Financial Post*, Nov. 20, 2012 (accessed April 1, 2017). Available at http://business.financialpost.com/executive/behind-the-scenes-of-td-canada-trusts-cultural-evolution.

The TD–Canada Trust merger illustrates the importance of a flexible strategic plan. This can and does happen. Strategy execution is a process that involves responding to problems as they arise. As much as the strategy may need to be tweaked to fit certain circumstances, other elements may need tweaking to better fit a changing strategy. Be flexible with the strategy, as well as with your values, culture, metrics and goals. While none of these pieces are fixed, they should all be aligned to your vision and strategic plan.

CHAPTER 10
THE SEVEN ELEMENTS OF STRATEGY EXECUTION: LEADERSHIP

Leaders' attitudes and behaviors are often identified as the most important factor in employee inspiration. A CEB Corporate Leadership Council study of fifty thousand employees in 59 countries revealed that, of the 160 drivers of engagement and retention, 22 of the top 25 drivers of employees' intentions to stay with the organization were leader-led.[108] Leaders are the key conduit for how an employee connects with their organization. It's leaders and managers who shape more positive, constructive behaviors in their teams.

From executives down, leaders demonstrate how they expect others to behave. They vocalize expectations, coach, teach and instruct. Leaders ensure that everyone, from executives to frontline employees, is investing in each other's success. They activate one another's skills. It's the difference between telling people "how things are done around here" to showing them "what is expected around here." Executives and managers must recognize that employees' leaders within are always listening and watching for behavioral cues. Just this understanding among leaders, an awareness of their impact on others, changes their behaviors as they pay more attention to the examples they're setting.

i) Leading by Example

---

[108] Corporate Leadership Council, "Driving Performance and Retention Through Employee Engagement: A Quantitative Analysis of Effective Engagement Strategies," 2004 (accessed May 15, 2017). Available at http://cwfl.usc.edu/assets/pdf/Employee%20engagement.pdf.

For all the positive influence leaders can wield, they can also negatively impact culture when they set bad examples. Leaders must understand that all employees are observing them, their words and their actions. Managers may very well be unaware they are contributing to employee disengagement when they don't take action against passive or aggressive behaviors that hold back execution. Leaders have tremendously difficult jobs. They must be inspiring while always setting the right example. They must admit their mistakes and be honest with employees. They must foster positive, constructive work relationships between staff. They must be unceasing when it comes to culture. They must listen and inspire. Their natural talent, above all, should be managing and inspiring their team members.

Executives should be setting expectations for senior managers, who do the same for team leaders, and so on – all the way to frontline staff. Communication must be crystal clear so that nothing is lost in translation. It's frontline staff – your tellers, sales representatives, customer service agents, baristas – who are executing the strategy. Even executives should have direct contact with the front line to directly impart the culture and behaviors. All leaders must understand that excited and inspired leaders within hold the keys to the kingdom. It's the job of leaders to bring out these leaders within by setting and maintaining expectations. When you embolden leaders within you create a high-performance organization that exceeds expectations and executes the strategy consistently, week to week and year to year.

What does it mean to set an example? As Curt Coffman and Kathie Sorenson write in their book about culture, leaders must get their hands dirty.[109] When they see a process that isn't right, one that's not quite aligned with the culture, they should identify it and help improve it. If a structure is out of alignment, they should reorganize it to reinforce the ideal culture that's been established and communicated. When a leader sees another manager who's setting the wrong example, behaviors should be corrected. When a manager or team member is the

---

[109] Curt W. Coffman and Kathie Sorenson, *Culture Eats Strategy for Lunch,* 151.

wrong fit and can't get on board with the strategy or the culture, a leader should get their hands dirty: It's time for that difficult conversation. Getting your hands dirty is a way of showing team members that you're one of them, that you're in this with them. It's showing them, not telling them, what's expected to advance the strategy.

ii) How to Empower a Team

Leaders carry a majority of the responsibility for their organizational culture. It's critical to understand this from the outset because employees are unlikely to improve or change a company's culture on their own. Employees don't fail on their own. In fact, consider it your fault if, as a manager or executive, you haven't helped your team succeed. Leaders need to own this role. A leader who blames their team members for failure has no business being a manager.[110] The leader's job is to empower their team members, giving them responsibilities, trust and independence, and then holding them accountable. They inform team members why they're doing what they're doing so that team members can make their own independent decisions to get the job done. A leader shares knowledge and sets the tone. They give team members direction, training and resources to accomplish their goals.[111] The tone, the behaviors you want from your employees, starts at the top.

Leaders need to empower each and every one of their team members. The 20th-century's "compliance" approach to motivating staff – where carrots (monetary rewards) are dangled in front of staff – is no longer appropriate in today's working environment.[112] Employees are smarter than previous generations, hold higher standards and expect much more from their workplaces. They must feel personal fulfillment at work; good leaders help them find this. As a leader, see yourself as a helper, coach and protector – not a commander. Offer encour-

---

[110] Paul L. Marciano, *Carrots and Sticks Don't Work,* 151.
[111] Simon Sinek, *Leaders Eat Last,* 145–6.
[112] Daniel H. Pink, *Drive,* 111.

aging, positive feedback regularly, if not constantly. Employees need regular confidence boosts, the rush of serotonin that comes with positive feedback. People are ultimately social and want to feel they are doing something of value. And they are, so show them. Leaders reward employees by communicating their value, supporting them in their goals and helping them find purpose in their work.

Leaders foster accountability. Employees and leaders hold one another accountable. The team member does not want to let the others down – and vice versa.[113] Leaders establish ground rules that encourage people to speak up and engage in open discussion. One ground rule may be to encourage open discussion about issues, not personalities, and tell employees to save their water-cooler gossip for a meeting. You want to hear it all. They should feel free to openly communicate what they think about decisions, processes and the culture.[114] Do they see any problems? And how is their team executing? Is it ahead or behind in meeting its targets, and why?

Increase employee ownership over tasks and their confidence and autonomy in decisions. Employees should feel that the organization, in a very public way, recognizes their work – perhaps on the company website or in internal newsletters. Give them something to be proud of. You may recognize employees through gifts to them or their families. Team members experience a feeling of pride when their families are shown how much their work is appreciated. Some companies, for a new hire, invite the family for a tour of the office, and send flowers or cookies to the spouse. Or they may send a gift basket or card to the spouse after the team member has put in extra time on a project, or send gifts to employees' children.[115] Don't forget to involve employees in decisions. Leaders should seek team members' input at meetings and critical junctures, such as

---

[113] Simon Sinek, *Leaders Eat Last,* 48.
[114] Roger Connors and Tom Smith, *Change the Culture, Change the Game*, 127.
[115] Ron Friedman, *The Best Place to Work: The Art and Science of Creating an Extraordinary Workplace* (New York: Penguin Group, 2014), 258.

during changes to the organizational culture, values, vision, strategy or goals. Be direct; ask for their honest opinions.

Good leaders identify champions. These may not necessarily be your top performers on the scorecard. Your champions, rather, are standout motivators who naturally promote the strategy and align themselves with the culture. They are genuine about the strategy, well-liked by colleagues, passionate facilitators of teamwork, and mediators when disagreements arise. Providing model behavior for others, they offer engaging, focused feedback that's positive and constructive.[116] Champions focus on strengths, minimize weaknesses and foster respect between colleagues. These are skills and capabilities that come naturally to some team members. It's important to identify them as champions and move them into appropriate roles. Perhaps this is facilitating meetings, organizing strategy-related events or sending daily results dashboards and newsletters about progress. You can't motivate the team and execute the strategy on your own. While leaders ensure teams are working together as smoothly as possible,[117] champions help fill in the gaps and smoothen the rough patches.

iii) Facilitative Leadership

As leaders, be facilitative. Facilitative leaders engage with the team members surrounding them. They facilitate employees' understanding of their value and their personal and career growth. They express a passionate inquisitiveness about what employees really think about an issue. Roger Connors and Tom Smith, in *Change the Culture, Change the Game*, say there are three questions leaders should consistently ask those they work with:

- What do you think?

- Why do you think it?

---

[116] Roger Connors and Tom Smith, *Change the Culture, Change the Game*, 129.
[117] Paul L. Marciano, *Carrots and Sticks Don't Work*, 134.

- What would you do?[118]

Asking and listening is one of the most important leadership behaviors when creating a high-performance culture. Managers can learn so much from their team members when they ask these questions honestly and – just as important – listen sincerely. Employees come away from these conversations feeling more valued and that they are making an important contribution. It's energizing for employees, for their leaders within, to have a "boss" who asks them for their opinions.

Facilitative leadership is the opposite to authoritative leadership. Instead of leading your team using fear tactics, lead them with enthusiasm and positivity, and help them problem-solve. It requires compassionate communication, particularly listening. Asking employees for their opinions – and asking what they would do in situations – does not necessarily mean they are giving actionable advice. Their comments should be discussed openly with other team members, so that, whatever decision comes out the other end, there is a feeling of group responsibility. The idea is not to implement all employee recommendations, but to listen to them and give them credit. Listening goes a long way to motivating employees by making them feel it is not the leader's project – it's everyone's.

Facilitative leadership comes back to open communications and trust. It means collaboration and group efforts to resolve conflicts. It means setting the tone for both passion and caring for team members and activating creativity and ownership of tasks. In the words of strategy coach Ken Todd Williams, the "practice of facilitative leadership establishes the conditions most conducive to the formation of bonds."[119] It's the difference between the authoritative leader who comes down with polarizing decisions versus the facilitative leader who encourages a healthy debate and discussion that opens up a clear path forward. Leaders who take this approach don't put team members in their place – they help them contribute.

---

[118] Roger Connors and Tom Smith, *Change the Culture, Change the Game,* 170.
[119] Ken Todd Williams, *The Practice of Facilitative Leadership* (Washington, D.C.: Laurel Wreath Strategies, 2013), 18.

CHAPTER 11
CHANGING THE CULTURE

At this point you may be recognizing that your organization has a culture that can be developed and shaped. You understand how the seven elements work together to engage a group of people and execute your plan. But execution cultures do not just happen on their own. They develop slowly as the behavior of every member of the group, especially its leaders, changes, and new expectations are set. Execution cultures have many parts that need to be actively shaped and monitored by management to ensure the success of the enterprise and those within it. Typically, an organization would require some outside help with managing this change and knowing where to start. Instead, take advantage of the expertise and direction outlined here for organizing and shaping an ideal culture

i) Assess

We hope that you now realize that you may be due for a culture change. Chances are, your organization needs one. But before making a change, you first have to understand what's holding back your execution. Leaders make an unfortunate mistake when they try to change the culture without understanding what's really going on among their people. Clever employee communications, PR campaigns, incentives and other attempts to direct the culture may be well-intentioned, but they are ultimately ineffective if they do not address underlying beliefs and behavior issues. In fact, such initiatives frequently trigger responses that undermine their intended purpose. Employees may dismiss the initiatives as blue-sky ideas or, worse, cynicism is furthered by sowing disagreement about the organization's goals.

So before you decide where you want to go, you first have to find out where you are. Leaders need a clear understanding of the obstacles standing in the way of teams and employees. What is getting in the way of alignment? What is holding back accountability? What's blocking goal attainment and personal success? Culture is often seen by leaders as abstract and difficult to connect to bottom-line results. It's commonly judged as soft. However you can get to the bottom of the attitudes and behaviors underlying your culture – the stuff thwarting results – if you measure correctly. Psychometric assessment tools can measure what subjective and qualitative surveys can't: They measure culture along many dimensions of behavior and attitudes. The data allows the organization to generate focused action plans for the company, leaders, managers, and project and work-group teams.

A culture assessment provides insight into employee beliefs and into their understanding of "what is expected around here." The assessment process usually begins by working with the organization's executives to identify the characteristics of their ideal organizational culture. From there, you proceed with an evaluation of the gap between the current and ideal culture. That starts with an investigation into the current culture – supported by deep research using direct reports and information from teams and employees – to see how people behave under the examples set by their leaders. The assessment can identify and quantify the attitudes and behaviors currently required to be successful at your organization. The findings are often surprising, showing a significant gap between the organization that leaders actually have and the one they think they have.

Psychometric assessment tools are the starting point. They chart a course from the organization's current culture to its ideal one. The assessment identifies the "missing link" for organizations, enabling leaders to see where employees are coming from, whether any constructive expectations are working and whether employees see any barriers getting in the way of their best work. What is it in your culture that prevents team members from speaking up? What is it about your culture that shuts down their drive? By identifying the behavioral issues getting in the way of execution, you are isolating the gap between your organization's current and ideal culture. With the gap identified, you have an opportunity to close it.

While other metrics are available, we recommend assessment tools developed by Human Synergistics International. They incorporate the Circumplex into their assessments, such as the Organizational Culture Inventory®, Life Styles Inventory™, Group Styles Inventory™, and Customer Service Styles™. This visual model helps develop the Constructive styles in individuals, managers, leaders, teams, and organizations.

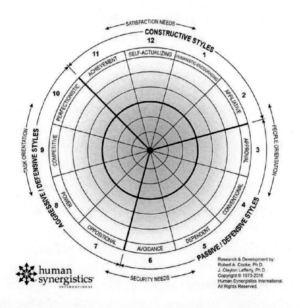

The circumplex breaks down the factors underlying performance effectiveness according to three general clusters and 12 behaviors. The three clusters include:

- Constructive styles that encourage the attainment of organizational goals through people development; promote teamwork and synergy; and enhance individual, group, and organizational adaptability and effectiveness.

- Aggressive/Defensive styles that lead people to focus on their own needs at the expense of those of their group and organization and lead to stress, turnover, and inconsistent performance.

- Passive/Defensive styles that lead people to subordinate themselves to the organization, stifle creativity and initiative, and allow the organization to stagnate.

Under each of the clusters there are four behaviors:

- Constructive Style includes Achievement, Self-Actualizing, Humanistic-Encouraging and Affiliative

- Passive/Defensive Style includes Approval, Conventional, Dependent and Avoidance

- Aggressive/Defensive Style include Oppositional, Power, Competitive and Perfectionistic.

Blue, green, and red extensions on the Circumplex graphically depict statistical results and the styles' strength in terms of percentile scores — so you can see how your individual, group, or organizational results compare with those of thousands of other organizations that we've already researched.

The firm's Organizational Culture Inventory (OCI) is one of our primary instruments for measuring culture and providing deep insight into the attitudes, beliefs and behaviors influencing an organization's culture and performance. The tool allows you to analyze the current culture, identify your ideal culture and help you plan how to get there. It can provide the organization with a snapshot of subgroup cultures, potentially extending culture analyses to a group of leaders and managers, a business unit, a team, a location or even a subgroup for your top talent.

For other metrics, we use the Life Styles Inventory to assess individuals, the Leadership/Impact tool to assess leaders, and the Group Styles Inventory to assess teams. We use these tools, developed by Human Synergistics, because we've seen their results firsthand. The assessments enable leaders to see where key roles, teams, people, behaviors and relationships are misaligned – and how they can be brought into alignment.

The OCI assessment provides answers to questions such as:

- What are the underpinnings of a culture that generates extraordinary results?

- What is supporting (and what is hindering) the creation of a high-performance culture?

- What is the ideal culture profile for the organization (or department or group)?

- What is its current operating culture?

- How is the current culture affecting the group's performance?

- How can the organization be a great place to work, attracting and retaining the right people?

- How can the group increase collaboration, knowledge sharing and innovation?

- What will it take to change the culture, and what type of leadership is needed?

- How can the culture be resilient or strengthened in times of change or chaos?

In this initial assessment phase, the organization sets up an Ideal and Current website to serve as a single entry point for the culture-change process. Basic employee data is collected (name and email) to establish initial lists for assessments and communication. Interviews then proceed with the leadership team, and emails are sent to employees to start assessing the culture. Human Synergistics 12 aspects of behavioral norms and values are compared against the behavioral norms, attitudes and values held by members of the organization. Employees can pick specific groups they belong to (however they can opt out) to gather organizational data.

After interviews are conducted and the results analyzed, a survey analysis is delivered and presented to executives. This assessment phase typically takes four to six weeks.

At the end of the assessment phase, you should arrive at outcomes such as:

- The identification of an ideal culture profile.

- A detailed understanding of the current culture and how and where it's holding back alignment, aspirations, values and change.

- An analysis of how and where the current culture may be hindering organizational agility and work with business partners.

- An understanding of how the current culture is holding back career excitement, attracting and retaining talent and striking a balance between the vision, strategy and day-to-day tasks.

- Knowledge of what you need to do to engage employees and create a great place to work.

ii) Design

Now that you've put your finger on it and know what your culture is, you can do something about it. Finally, there is a feeling that the thing that seemed to be perpetually elusive – high performance – can be grasped. It's time to start working toward where you want to go, bringing you to the second phase: design. This is the creation of a detailed plan to work toward your ideal behaviors and beliefs. We'll call it your culture strategy. There are two steps in this phase, which generally takes about four weeks: first, strategy sessions and workshops to discuss the culture, and second, assessing the impact of leaders.

The strategy sessions start with further debriefings with leaders and their teams to discuss the findings of the culture survey. A series of culture strategy sessions are recommended with the leadership team to create a focused plan to bridge the gap from your current culture to your ideal profile. These are action-learning sessions with leaders, where leaders discuss the culture and the behaviors they want. They also discuss the tools and incentives they can use to draw model behaviors out from employees. The culture strategy sessions demystify culture for leaders, enabling them to fully understand the outsized impact leaders and executives have on employees.

Separately, it's important to hold a workshop that involves all leaders in the organization, to hash out a culture strategy plan. The leaders together identify their ideal constructive culture within the cultural inventory and come up with a road map to get there. Your organization must have in place a well-developed vision, strategy and goals – because the ideal culture will need to be in alignment with these. The culture strategy should cover everything from programs and resources to processes and rewards. Consider specific programs for leadership and coaching. Leaders will need to design programs and processes for feedback, teamwork and collaboration, training, events and information sessions. Establish a process for how the cultural transformation will be communicated – perhaps through newsletters, blogs, webinars and information sessions. A regular support group should be set up, perhaps monthly, to answer questions from team members and share successes as the transformation progresses.

Following the strategy sessions and workshops, leaders should be able to recognize the desired patterns and behaviors of the ideal culture and contrast them with the current culture. There may be some, indeed many, activities the company has been running that align perfectly with the ideal culture profile. It's important to identify these and continue them. At the same time, leaders should identify the activities, programs and behaviors that no longer work, and come up with a plan to cease those operations and communicate the details of these changes to team members. The workshops, overall, should feel therapeutic. They should be an intensive learning and sharing experience from which the leaders emerge sensing they have created something new together.

As the culture strategy plan is being finalized, leaders need to better understand their individual impacts. A big part of changing your culture is addressing the influence of leaders on an individual level. They need to know whether what they're doing, and how they're doing it, is advancing the culture, vision and strategy. To do this, we recommend using an assessment tool called Leadership Impact, also by Human Synergistics. The tool provides further data illustrating that leaders are the primary drivers of constructive cultures that make things happen. Executives and leaders in the organization must understand their impact on the culture and embrace the responsibility. They must own the duty to influence how their people approach their work and interact with each other. After running the Leadership Impact tool, leaders will better understand how they're affecting performance and see which actions and activities are having a positive or negative impact. They will see which of their own behaviors, activities and processes encourage people to compete versus cooperate.

The Leadership Impact tool includes a self-assessment as well as a questionnaire that is to be completed by up to five of the leader's senior managers or direct reports. Quite different from traditional 360-degree assessments, the Leadership Impact assessment singles out the impact of a person's leadership style on the behaviors and attitudes of staff, rather than providing just a performance and competency assessment. Leaders are often surprised when they learn the impact of their influence. Leaders not only see the ripple effects of their working styles, they also come to understand the effectiveness of their leadership style on their department or organization. Leaders will understand what they're doing right in creating their desired culture, and what's counterproductive. At the end of the assessment process, they should receive direction for further development of their leadership skills and competencies.

iii) Implement

With a culture strategy in place, it's time to implement. The implementation phase is focused on launching the projects, programs and other actions of the culture strategy plan. It will feel like a big undertaking, especially if the culture change is happening alongside a change in strategy for the organization. But you can't lose sight of the culture goal, which should happen first. You don't want to start executing before you're ready to perform. The strategic plan and the culture goal are perfectly aligned, and a culture transformation is a wonderful opportunity to communicate the strategy at every turn.

Leaders should get their hands dirty as they help implement the culture strategy. They should work with teams to figure out the practical details of new programs and actions – and ensure they are adjusting them to be in alignment. They analyze any barriers and misalignment presented in the metrics. Are you measuring the outcomes and behaviors you want? Are metrics and reward systems aligned with the strategy and the culture profile? Working directly with teams, your employees and steering committees help with the implementation and recommend key changes to the organization's metrics and processes.

Leaders, who are not only managing change to organizational infrastructure but also their own leadership style, must continue to receive coaching (internal or external resource) through this process. Coaching sessions should be available to leaders regularly and by request. Offer leaders information kits that answer tailored FAQs, such as their role in the culture change, why it's important, and when and how they should get involved in addressing behaviors and the culture.

Employees should know what their role is in the culture change and how they can get involved and make an impact. They should understand why it's important. They should be able to clearly see their role within the team, offer suggestions, and help and support their colleagues. For instance, if they see a colleague struggling in a meeting or presentation, they can support the colleague in the moment. They know positive feedback, and an environment that encourages this, is part of the culture going forward. Also important, employees should form a culture team to work on culture-building activities, such as creating newsletters, posters, information sessions, clubs and charity events. Composed of nonmanagement employees, the culture team presents these activities and progress reports to management on a regular basis. It's a great motivator and employee-engagement system supporting the change.

Mentoring is also a useful function in change management. Offer mentoring dates with a leader through coffees, lunches or coaching and mentoring sessions. Leaders can talk to team members about the culture change and discuss examples of how to work through certain situations or problems. Coffee dates with an executive could also be offered, where the culture goal and the new strategy are discussed. Throughout the implementation, management should articulate the key roles of employees in changing the culture and assessing the impact that leaders, staff and teams are having on the ideal and current cultures. Results of the culture assessments – including where the organization is at in relation to its culture goal – should be shared with all employees to build buy-in and encourage everyone to join the push for change.

Transforming culture is not easy. Some team members and leaders may need to change. Not everyone will be on board with the culture and the strategy; when that's the case, it's time to reach an agreement with the stubborn non–team players. They have to understand that they're not a good fit. Cutting ties with team members is never easy but it may need to happen – just as leaders may need to revisit processes, structures, programs and the rest of the organizational infrastructure. Leaders, coached through these changes, will have the ability to recognize whether something is out of alignment.

iv) Communicate

No strategy will succeed without excellent communications. In the same way, culture change can't happen without exceptional communications. Your communications plan for the culture change may also be thought of as translation. Communicating the change is translating the culture strategy into actionable items for teams and employees. Strategy sessions should be held with the organization's operational teams while employees hold group sessions to discuss the culture and behaviors – and what needs to change.

Emphasis in the communication phase is placed on educating executives and leaders about the change and the path ahead. Executives and leaders should receive regular, focused feedback throughout the process and teams should, at minimum, receive a half-day feedback retreat followed by a half-day action-planning session.

In some cases, it's recommended that the organization run the Life Styles Inventory and Group Styles Inventory assessments. These tools by Human Synergistics provide insight into how your people interact with one another and engage with one another to problem-solve, at both a group and individual level. The assessments are a jumping-off point for employees to talk about behaviors and to understand how they affect performance. Open group conversations are empowering for employees, and in this case they give them focal points for behavioral changes aligned with the strategy and the ideal culture. In these sessions, teams should develop action plans at each level to integrate their ideal culture profile into everyday practices and programs.

Sessions are also held to discuss individual leadership (leaders within), competencies and the short-term goals needed to ensure personal, team and organizational success. The strategy sessions start to activate accountability in individuals and teams, enhance cooperation, build trust and form the underpinning of the new culture. Employees learn how to empower their leader within, take ownership of their work and establish personal action plans.

After teams understand the culture strategy, all teams in the transformation (for example, the organization or department) must receive the current culture profile results so they understand what culture they have now. The ideal culture that they're working toward must also be explained – they need to understand not only that there's a gap but also what the gap is. In a group setting, articulate this cultural gap and outline what the group's core purpose and aspirations are in the transformation. They should understand what they need to do in a practical way, in on-the-job terms. The transformation and culture strategy is communicated down through leaders to team members at all levels. They are told why they are doing this. This is not just another corporate directive from on high. Employees should feel that the change is positive, ambitious, smart and necessary.

They clearly see the difference between constructive behaviors (innovation, big-picture thinking, collaboration, healthy competitiveness, goal orientation) and defensive or aggressive behaviors (excessive conformance to rules, silo mentalities, wait-to-be-told attitudes). They understand the role of leaders and individuals. They understand their own impact on a personal level. They see culture as a key business measure linked to the strategy. Engaging your people in the culture strategy is important for the same reason it's important you engage them in the development of your overall strategy, vision and goals. People need to feel they are given a voice. Do this by providing mechanisms for simple, anonymous input about the current culture, and again during the transformational phase, which works the attitudes and behaviors of the ideal culture into the day-to-day job. It's not enough for leaders to discuss among themselves which behaviors match the ideal culture.

Through this process, the organization should be providing support to employees as it communicates the "intangibles" of changing the culture. Regular communications, meetings, even hotlines and points of contact are necessary to answer any questions. Excellent communications should include the how and the why – for example, why measurement and some processes are changing, why certain behaviors are expected, what's being changed to align with the strategy or why the president of the division is now holding office hours – will help translate the big longer-term goals into day-to-day tasks. Communications with employees and teams reinforce your culture strategy imperatives: What are the results to be achieved and what are the attitudes and behaviors necessary to achieve them?

Identify and relay the key messages you want to convey about the culture and repeat them. A common yet simple way to communicate the change is to talk about how the group is making improvements on "the way we work around here." In your messages, include themes about the culture and its alignment with the vision. Help team members understand how everything in the organization should be aligned with the vision and strategy and encourage them to challenge behaviors or processes that stray. The quantitative (surveys and assessments) and qualitative (behaviors) information you provide can serve as objective conversation starters for teams at all levels. Be sure to align internal and external brands in this process – or employees will see the disconnect. All of the language in your communications, internal and external, should reflect your vision, strategy and ideal culture.

Constant communication about the culture change at and between all levels is vital. Leaders must understand how each decision is interpreted. "Decision meter" communications are also useful for employees to help them understand each decision – how and why it's being made. Executives should offer regular information sessions about how the transformation is going, perhaps through monthly video messages or teleconferences, supplemented by email, messaging platforms and social media posts. Offer these in a single-page handout or short email. It's useful to offer regular round tables throughout the change, where employees can discuss and share what's working, what's not working and any unexpected challenges. Create a feedback mechanism for frontline staff – this is especially important for those who are farther away from head office. It's vital to hear about how the culture change is going on the front lines in all regions. Digital suggestion boxes are another available tool, as well as a hotline that staff can call to receive tips and feedback and advice. Employees should feel they have a mentor or leader they can reach out to for any questions and advice. You might offer opportunities to meet with senior people, perhaps a meeting or breakfast with a division chief or director. All these communications reinforce your goal: to align with the strategy while transforming the culture.

v) Progress Assessment

Along the way, the culture should be assessed to determine whether you're on track. This second assessment should be similar to the first using the same tools and processes. The re-measuring should usually happen within 12 to 18 months of the original culture assessment. Analyze the results to compare them against the organization's baseline for realigning the culture. This allows you to measure progress and again compare the current and ideal culture profiles. The reassessment will reveal what we call "pulse checks" – how the culture has shifted.

Based on this reassessment, start to adjust activities, processes and behaviors based on where you see gaps. For instance, if your metrics are causing some unintended, unwanted behaviors, some adjustment is necessary. At this point, it is important to follow up on the impact of leaders and managers. What impacts have they had, and where has the culture change been weakened? Efforts can be put into improving any weak spots that deserve more attention – perhaps with specific geographic regions farther from head office or in a department where culture leadership is lacking. The reassessment will identify these gaps and you can rerun the same implementation process to address them. Remember that your culture is fluid and always evolving. It needs constant attention and upkeep to shape it into one that performs best.

vi) Refine

Organizational culture should not be left to the powers of entropy. Cultures evolve, and your people must be continually reminded of what's expected of them if your organization is seeking performance, results and execution. The refine phase, the final step in cultural transformation, addresses any gaps in knowledge transfer and puts processes in place to ensure the culture is taught, spread and sustained. Create a working group on knowledge transfer so that there is a process embedded into the organization to show new employees what's expected. Hold sessions for employees that discuss how to informally train new colleagues on the culture. Continue the work of the in-house organizational culture team, made up of nonmanagement employees, and give them a mandate to hold leaders accountable for their commitments to change the culture. The culture team should be constantly observing the behaviors of leaders and the impacts of organizational infrastructure so that adjustments can be made where necessary.

As part of the efforts to refine the culture, some key messages and best practices may include:

- The concept of the leader within is foundational to culture change. The individual has the power to change what gets done, what is executed. You can't change others, you can change only yourself.

- Culture is built on behaviors. Often, an organization's focus is on processes and policy because it's easier and more comfortable to talk about and address. We must remind ourselves that our actions, over time, build the behaviors that make up a constructive culture.

- Culture should be embedded in your language, behaviors and actions – and in everything you do at every level. Culture is inherently important to the success of your organization and it should be treated accordingly. As you make decisions, ensure your communications to employees and the organization relay the correct message. Interpret the impact of each message and each decision. If you don't know, ask.

- Whatever you put your attention on grows stronger. What gets measured is what matters and what gets done.

Remind yourself that employees should be involved in the culture transformation, helping to develop action plans and culture strategies they can share with the group. Team members at all levels should be aware of their responsibility to hold leadership accountable. The culture team takes responsibility for making new commitments to drive culture with a focus on engagement, retention and inspiration, for both the people and the business. Employees may create intention statements (what behaviors they will need to change) to bring out their own leaders within. They should be encouraged to take notes to reflect on meetings and behaviors they observe. Employees should be given roles within the culture change. Perhaps a person or group is tasked with creating a hotline, so team members can call in to share good news and opportunities for improvement. Maybe other team members take up the job of creating a bulletin or newsletter highlighting constructive behaviors, illustrated by blog posts, cartoons, a reading or a quotation.

Continued coaching, reassessment or even interventions may be necessary along the way to deal with gaps. It's important to revisit organizational systems, infrastructure and branding to ensure everything and everyone within the group is aligned with the ideal culture and the vision and strategy. The refine phase is ongoing. Like muscles, the organizational culture needs regular exercise to remain strong. Organizations and their leaders should never rest from shaping and improving their cultures.

CONCLUSION

Culture does not change overnight. Culture change is a fundamental organizational transformation, requiring diligence, persistence, measurement and discussion. It's a change requiring leaders to consistently show model behavior. Transforming your culture is not a project. It is an ongoing mindset and a way of doing business that balances the very human nature of organizations with achievement and a focus on strategic objectives. Depending on an organization's current culture profile, significant, measurable improvement in culture may take a year or more. The change begins with what we call the courageous conversation: first, a conversation with yourself as a leader confronting current behaviors; second, a discussion with others about how the change can happen.

As noted at the start of this book, strategies too often get shelved because they don't progress. And it's not for lack of a great strategy. It's because the execution part is missing. The results of a high-performance culture speak for themselves: where your strategy execution exceeds expectations. Employees are motivated and engaged, and teams run in a more focused and efficient way. Your workforce is not looking for opportunities elsewhere; they're motivated to take on the next challenge. You have employee buy-in. Successful implementation of strategy is a near certainty.

Your culture is the missing link between your strategic plan and its outcomes becoming reality. If you're debating whether you need a culture change, think about what may be holding back execution by considering the following questions:

- What's currently driving your business: beliefs and behaviors aligned with goals? Or fear?

- Do your people offer little more than letter-of-the-law compliance with their job descriptions and functions?

- Are your people engaged not just rationally – but emotionally?

- Do team members invest discretionary effort and undertake decision-making to get results? Or do they have wait-to-be-told attitudes?

- Are your organization's behaviors aligned with your best interests and strategic objectives? Are rewards, values, vision and strategy aligned?

- Are the principles of accountability, transparency and task ownership expressed and understood throughout the organization?

- Do employees have a clear line of sight on their goals and the organization's strategy and values?

- Do your people collaborate and share ideas across departments and sections? Or are there silos and turf protection?

- Do employees feel supported and that they are achieving personal success?

These are difficult questions, we know. The answers may not be very comforting – especially if you're already aware that your organization has a habit of failing to execute strategy. But standout execution is possible for your organization. We've outlined here the seven essential ingredients to make strategy execution happen: clarity, commitment, the team, accountability, synergy, the plan and leadership.

The final element is vital. We can't stress enough the importance of having tremendous leaders. On an individual level, each of them must be an excellent fit with the ideal culture you're trying to achieve. They should sustain positive, constructive attitudes, seeing the glass half full. They have a healthy relationship with uncertainty, doubt and failure, seeing fear as a driver rather than an impediment. They have great judgment and see what motivates each of their team members. They know it takes time to execute strategy and goals, and are not rushed to make important decisions. They have an inspired relationship with employees, customers, shareholders and stakeholders. They are inspired by honesty and truth, showing trust in their teams and employees – and vice versa.

Organizations that successfully foster high-performance cultures understand that the culture is not static – no culture is. They build an organizational culture that's constantly evolving, cultivating itself and striving to be better. Employees are aware of the ideal culture and talk regularly about behaviors and attitudes. There is innovation in thinking and doing, professional development for individuals and teams, and an emphasis on collaboration. Everyone is investing in each other's success.

These organizations recognize culture as a key business measure – just like production or sales. It is a day-to-day consideration for teams and individuals. People are given a voice and feel they have influence. They are enriching the traditional workplace notion of "what we need to accomplish" with "how we need to work." Your organization can be a high performer, too. Lead the growth of a passionate, focused and engaged team – working within an inspiring culture – and you'll enable breakthrough strategy execution.

ABOUT THE AUTHORS

 **Mona Mitchell** is President and CEO of ACHIEVEBLUE™. Mona's expertise includes working with global organizations' executive teams to develop high performing environments. Her work related to self, team and enterprise effectiveness enables these organizations and their employees to thrive and excel. Mona has over thirty years of industry experience in business development, management, leadership and talent development. She is an executive coach, facilitator and professional speaker.

Mona's passion extends to giving back with a focus on women and children's not-for-profit organizations. As a board member and executive coach, she contributes to their success by mentoring the leadership team in the areas of strategy and organizational effectiveness.

Mona can be reached at mmitchell@achieveblue.com. ACHIEVEBLUE's website is www.achieveblue.com

David Barrett is a professional speaker, regular blogger, podcast host, author of 5 books and education advisor. He specializes in helping people and organizations 'Manage the Uncertainty' by creating healthy projects and strategies.

David has been in the business of project management since 1997. He is the founder and past Managing Director of ProjectWorld, ProjectSummit and BusinessAnalystWorld conferences held around the world. He is the National Program Director for all Project Management training out of the Schulich Executive Education Centre, Schulich School of Business, York University and in partnership with nine other universities across Canada.

He is the founder and past Executive Director of ProjectTimes.com.

David has held board positions for numerous charitable and not-for-profit organizations.

David's web site is www.DavidBarrett.ca

He can be reached at dbarrett@solutionsnetwork.com

REFERENCES

8. Gary L. Neilson, Karla L. Martin and Elizabeth Powers, "The Secrets to Successful Strategy Execution," *Harvard Business Review*, June 2008 (accessed July 12, 2017). Available at https://hbr.org/2008/06/the-secrets-to-successful-strategy-execution.

13. Ann Barnes President and CEO MedData, interview with authors (October 2017).

20. The Conference Board Ben Cheng, Michelle Kan, Gad Levanon, Ph.D., and Rebecca L. Ray, Ph.D. as per www.conference-board.org/publications/publicationdetail.cfm?publicationid=2785&centerId=4?], "Job Satisfaction: 2014 Edition," The Conference Board, June 2014 (accessed March 15, 2017). Available at www.conference-board.org/publications/publicationdetail.cfm?publicationid=2785.

22. Victor Tan, "Benefits of Corporate Culture," *New Straits Times*, July 20, 2002.

22. Daniel H. Pink, *Drive: The Surprising Truth about What Motivates Us* (New York: Riverhead Books, 2011).

23. Zeynep Ton, *The Good Jobs Strategy: How the Smartest Companies Invest in Employees to Lower Costs and Boost Profits ("New York: Houghton Mifflin" 2014).*
23. Emma Seppälä and Kim Cameron, "Proof That Positive Work Cultures Are More Productive," *Harvard Business Review,* Dec. 1, 2015 (accessed March 10, 2017). Available at https://hbr.org/2015/12/proof-that-positive-work-cultures-are-more-productive.

24. Emma Seppälä and Kim Cameron, "Proof That Positive Work Cultures Are More Productive."

24. Ann Barnes President and CEO MedData, interview with the authors (October 2017)

25. Chris McChesney, Sean Covey and Jim Huling, *The 4 Disciplines of Execution: Achieving Your Wildly Important Goals* (New York: Franklin Covey Co., 2012).

26. Martha Lagace, "Gerstner: Changing Culture at IBM - Lou Gerstner Discusses Changing the Culture at IBM," *HBS Working Knowledge*, Sept. 12, 2002 (accessed March 20, 2017). Available at http://hbswk.hbs.edu/archive/3209.html; see also Louis V. Gerstner, Jr., *Who Says Elephants Can't Dance? Leading a Great Enterprise through Dramatic Change* (New York: Harper Business, 2002).

29. Edgar H. Schein, *Organizational Culture and Leadership*, 4th ed. (San Francisco: Jossey-Bass, 2010).

38. Brian Solis, "Zappos' Tony Hsieh Delivers Happiness Through Service and Innovation," BrianSolis.com, April 11, 2011 (accessed April 12, 2017). Available at www.briansolis.com/2011/04/zappos-tony-hsieh-happiness.

39. Cynthia Johnson, "Generation Z and the Future of Business," *Entrepreneur*, March 3, 2017 (accessed April 22, 2017). Available at www.entrepreneur.com/article/289847.

39. https://www.ft.com/content/96187a7a-fce5-11e6-96f8-3700c5664d30 Philosopher Daniel Dennett on AI, robots and religion

44. Paul L. Marciano, *Carrots and Sticks Don't Work: Building a Culture of Employee Engagement with the R.E.S.P.E.C.T. Principle* (New York: McGraw-Hill, 2010), 152.

46. Stephen Gunn, Sleep Country Canada, interview with the authors (August 2016).

46. Robert MacLellan, former TD executive, interview with the authors (March 2016).

46. Robert MacLellan, former TD executive, interview with the authors (March 2016).

47. Robert MacLellan, former TD executive, interview with the authors (March 2016).

47. Chris Nickerson, senior vice president, sales and, NEI Investments, interview with the authors (October 2016).

48. David Hopkinson, chief commercial officer, Maple Leaf Sports & Entertainment, interview with the authors (December 2014).

48. David Hopkinson, chief commercial officer, Maple Leaf Sports & Entertainment, interview with the authors (December 2014).

49. Robert MacLellan, former TD executive, interview with the authors (March 2016).

49. Daniel H. Pink, *Drive: The Surprising Truth about What Motivates Us* (New York: Riverhead Books, 2009).

50. Daniel H. Pink, *Drive: The Surprising Truth about What Motivates Us* (New York: Riverhead Books, 2009).

53. Chris Nickerson, senior vice president, sales distribution and marketing, NEI Investments, interview with the authors (October 2016).

54. David Hopkinson, chief commercial officer, Maple Leaf Sports & Entertainment, interview with the authors (December 2014).

54. Michael Schrage, "Reward Your Best Teams, Not Just Star Players," *Harvard Business Review*, June 30, 2015 (accessed March 18, 2017). Available at https://hbr.org/2015/06/reward-your-best-teams-not-just-star-players.

55. Daniel H. Pink, *Drive: The Surprising Truth about What Motivates Us* (New York: Riverhead Books, 2009).

55. *Harvard Business Review. Katherine Bell interview with Daniel H. Pink*, Feb. 18, 2010 (accessed Dec. 3, 2016). Available at https://hbr.org/2010/02/what-motivates-us

56. Ann Barnes, President & CEO MedData, interview with the authors (October 2017).

57. Art Markman, "Your Employees' Emotions Are Clues to What Motivates Them," *Harvard Business Review*, May 18, 2015 (accessed June 2, 2017). Available at https://hbr.org/2015/05/your-employees-emotions-are-clues-to-what-motivates-them.

58. Robert A. Cooke and Linda Sharkey, "Developing Constructive Leader Impact," *Consulting Today,* 2006 (accessed Nov. 13, 2016). Available at www.humansynergistics.com/Files/ResearchAndPublications/Consulting_Today_Cooke_Sharkey_Constructive_Leader_Impact.pdf

58. Robert A. Cooke and Linda Sharkey, "Developing Constructive Leader Impact," *Consulting Today,* 2006 (accessed Nov. 13, 2016). Available at www.humansynergistics.com/Files/ResearchAndPublications/Consulting_Today_Cooke_Sharkey_Constructive_Leader_Impact.pdf

59. Robert A. Cooke and Linda Sharkey, "Developing Constructive Leader Impact," *Consulting Today,* 2006 (accessed Nov. 13, 2016). Available at ww.humansynergistics.com/Files/ResearchAndPublications/Consulting_Today_Cooke_Sharkey_Constructive_Leader_Impact.pdf.

62. Larry Bossidy, Ram Charan and Charles Burck, *Execution: The Discipline of Getting Things Done* (New York: Crown Business, 2002), 129–30.

62. David Hopkinson, chief commercial officer, Maple Leaf Sports & Entertainment, interview with the authors (December 2014).

62. Greg McKeown, "Hire Slow, Fire Fast," *Harvard Business Review,* March 3, 2014 (accessed May 20, 2017). Available at https://hbr.org/2014/03/hire-slow-fire-fast.

63. David Hopkinson, chief commercial officer, Maple Leaf Sports & Entertainment, interview with the authors (December 2014).

63. Stephen Gunn, Sleep Country Canada, interview with the authors (August 2016).

64. William S. Schaninger, Jr., Stanley G. Harris and Robert E. Niebuhr, "Adapting General Electric's Workout for Use in Other Organizations: A Template," *Manage-*

ment Development Forum, vol. 2, No. 1, 1999 (accessed April 1, 2017). Available at www8.esc.edu/ESConline/Across_ESC/forumjournal.nsf/0/c8c020477ee750cb8525 68fd0056cd61?OpenDocument

65. Chris Nickerson, senior vice president, sales distribution and marketing, NEI Investments, interview with the authors (October 2016).

65. Baldev Seekri, *Organizational Turnarounds with a Human Touch*: Trafford Publishing, 2011), 155–60

66. Patrick M. Lencioni, *Silos, Politics and Turf War: A Leadership Fable about Destroying the Barriers that Turn Colleagues into Competitors* (San Francisco: Jossey-Bass, 2006).

66. Patrick M. Lencioni, "Author Q & A Pat Lencioni - Silos, Politics and Turf Wars," The Table Group, 2014 (accessed April 16, 2017). Available at www.tablegroup.com/imo/media/doc/Author_QandA_Pat_Lencioni_Silos_Politics %20and%20Turf%20Wars.pdf.

67. Andrew Hill, "It Is Time to Kill the Org Chart," *Financial Times*, Dec. 12, 2016 (accessed April 30, 2017). Available at www.ft.com/content/2a477ad6-bc98-11e6-8b45-b8b81dd5d080

67. See www.holacracy.org

68. Zappos, "Holacracy and Self-Organization," Zappos Insights (accessed Dec. 18, 2016). Available at www.zapposinsights.com/about/holacracy.

68. Curt W. Coffman and Kathie Sorenson, *Culture Eats Strategy for Lunch: The Secret of Extraordinary Results, Igniting the Passion Within* (Denver, Colo.: Liang Addison Press, 2013), 66.

68. Glenn Kessler, "Do 10,000 Baby Boomers Retire Every Day?" *The Washington Post,* July 24, 2014 (accessed April 11, 2017). Available at www.washingtonpost.com/news/fact-checker/wp/2014/07/24/do-10000-baby-boomers-retire-every-day/?utm_term=.3fc70e7fe375

69. Dan Bursch and Kip Kelly, "Managing the Multigenerational Workplace," UNC Kenan-Flagler Business School, 2014 (accessed Jan. 28, 2017). Available at www.kenan-flagler.unc.edu/~/media/Files/documents/executive-development/managing-the-multigenerational-workplace-white-paper.pdf.

70. Glenn Rifkin, "Engaging the Multigenerational Workforce," *Briefings Magazine,* Korn Ferry Institute, Feb. 24, 2016 (accessed Jan. 28, 2017) Available at www.kornferry.com/institute/engaging-the-multigenerational-workforce.

73. Greg Bustin, *Accountability: The Key to Driving a High-Performance Culture* (New York: McGraw-Hill Education, 2014), 532.

74. James Heskett, *The Culture Cycle: How to Shape the Unseen Force That Transforms Performance* (Upper Saddle River, N.J.: FT Press, 2012), 181.

74. James Heskett, *The Culture Cycle,* 136–7.

74. Chris Nickerson, senior vice president, sales distribution and marketing, NEI Investments, interview with the authors (October 2016).

75. Simon Sinek, *Leaders Eat Last: Why Some Teams Pull Together and Others Don't* (New York: Portfolio / Penguin, 2014), 22.

76. Paul L. Marciano, *Carrots and Sticks Don't Work,* 121–2.

76. Greg Bustin, *Accountability,* 530.

76. Paul L. Marciano, *Carrots and Sticks Don't Work*, 122

77. Greg Bustin, *Accountability*, 650–1.

77. Paul L. Marciano, *Carrots and Sticks Don't Work*, 121–3; see also Don Clifton, *First, Break All the Rules: What the World's Greatest Managers Do Differently* (New York: Gallup Press, 2016), 247–8.

78. Paul L. Marciano, *Carrots and Sticks Don't Work*, 124.

78. Roger Connors and Tom Smith, *Change the Culture, Change the Game: The Breakthrough Strategy for Energizing Your Organization and Creating Accountability for Results* (New York: Penguin Group, Portfolio, 2011), 138–9.

79. Paul L. Marciano, *Carrots and Sticks Don't Work*, 149.

80. Greg Bustin, *Accountability*, 431–47.

81. Robert MacLellan, former TD executive, interview with the authors (March 2016).

81. Paul L. Marciano, *Carrots and Sticks Don't Work*, 152.

81. Chris McChesney, Sean Covey and Jim Huling, *The 4 Disciplines of Execution*, 80–1.

84. Ken Robertson, "Business Outcome Management," in David Barrett and Derek Vigar, Eds., *Keys to Our Success: Lessons Learned from 25 of Our Best Project Managers* (Oshawa, Ont.: Multi-Media Publications Inc., 2013), 167–77.

86. Paul L. Marciano, *Carrots and Sticks Don't Work,* 158.

86. Paul L. Marciano, *Carrots and Sticks Don't Work,* 159.

87. Liz Ryan, "How to Have Fun at Work," *Forbes.com,* Aug. 18, 2014 (accessed Jan. 18, 2017). Available at www.forbes.com/sites/lizryan/2014/08/18/how-to-have-fun-at-work/#6ada2fce73c9

87. Emma Seppälä, "Being Happier at Work," *Harvard Business Review,* Jan. 28, 2016 (accessed Jan. 18, 2017). Available at https://hbr.org/ideacast/2016/01/being-happier-at-work.

88. Robert A. Cooke and Linda Sharkey, "Developing Constructive Leader Impact."

88. Acqueline Whitmore, "The Surprising Benefits of Having Fun at Work," *Entrepreneur,* Jan. 31, 2017 (accessed March 4, 2017). Available at www.entrepreneur.com/article/288223.

88. Liz Ryan, "How to Have Fun at Work."

90. Perry Williams, "Musk Bets He Can Fix Aussie Power Woes in 100 Days or It's Free," Bloomberg News, March 10, 2017 (accessed March 19, 2017). Available at www.bloomberg.com/news/articles/2017-03-10/musk-bets-he-can-fix-aussie-power-woes-in-100-days-or-it-s-free.

92. Ashwin Srinivasan and Bryan Kurey, "Creating a Culture of Quality," *Harvard Business Review,* Apr. 2014 (accessed Oct. 1, 2016). Available at https://hbr.org/2014/04/creating-a-culture-of-quality.

92. Yvette Caslin, "Toyota Motor Manufacturing President Wil James Talks Culture and Employee Engagement," *Rollingout,* Apr. 8, 2013 (accessed Oct. 1, 2016). Available at http://rollingout.com/2013/04/08/toyota-motor-manufacturing-president-wil-james-talks-culture-and-employee-engagement.

93. Bossidy, Charan and Charles Burck, *Execution,* 148–9.

94. Paul L. Marciano, *Carrots and Sticks Don't Work,* 145–6.

94. Paul L. Marciano, *Carrots and Sticks Don't Work,* 145–9.

95. Paul L. Marciano, *Carrots and Sticks Don't Work,* 153.

95. Quoted in Simon Sinek, *Leaders Eat Last,* 43.

95. Daniel H. Pink, *Drive,* 165.

96. Daniel H. Pink, *Drive,* 49–50.

96. Build-A-Bear Workshop, "Why You Should Become a Bear" (accessed May 24, 2017). Available at https://careers.buildabear.com/AboutUs.aspx.

97. Whole Foods Market, "Our Core Values" (accessed May 24, 2017). Available at www.wholefoodsmarket.com/mission-values/core-values.

97. Daniel H. Pink, *Drive,* 142–5.

98. Paul L. Marciano, *Carrots and Sticks Don't Work,* 40–1.

99. Interview, McKinsey principals Wouter Aghina and Aaron De Smet, "The Keys to Organizational Agility," McKinsey & Company, December 2015 (accessed March 9, 2017). Available at www.mckinsey.com/business-functions/organization/our-insights/the-keys-to-organizational-agility.

100. Simon Sinek, *Leaders Eat Last,* 112–3.

100. Amanda Setili, *The Agility Advantage: How to Identify and Act on Opportunities in a Fast-Changing World* (San Francisco: John Wiley & Sons, 2014).

101. Robert MacLellan, former TD executive, interview with the authors (March 2016)

102. Robert MacLellan, former TD executive, interview with the authors (March 2016); see also Dan Ovsey, "Behind the Scenes of TD Canada Trust's Cultural Evolution," *Financial Post,* Nov. 20, 2012 (accessed April 1, 2017). Available at http://business.financialpost.com/executive/behind-the-scenes-of-td-canada-trusts-cultural-evolution.

103. Corporate Leadership Council, "Driving Performance and Retention Through Employee Engagement: A Quantitative Analysis of Effective Engagement Strategies," 2004 (accessed May 15, 2017). Available at http://cwfl.usc.edu/assets/pdf/Employee%20engagement.pdf.

104. Curt W. Coffman and Kathie Sorenson, *Culture Eats Strategy for Lunch,* 151.

105. Paul L. Marciano, *Carrots and Sticks Don't Work,* 151.

105. Simon Sinek, *Leaders Eat Last,* 145–6.

105. Daniel H. Pink, *Drive,* 111.

106. Simon Sinek, *Leaders Eat Last,* 48.

106. Roger Connors and Tom Smith, *Change the Culture, Change the Game*, 127.

107. Ron Friedman, *The Best Place to Work: The Art and Science of Creating an Extraordinary Workplace* (New York: Penguin Group, 2014), 258.

107. Roger Connors and Tom Smith, *Change the Culture, Change the Game*, 129.

107. Paul L. Marciano, *Carrots and Sticks Don't Work,* 134.
108. Roger Connors and Tom Smith, *Change the Culture, Change the Game,* 170.

109. Ken Todd Williams, *The Practice of Facilitative Leadership* (Washington, D.C.: Laurel Wreath Strategies, 2013), 18.